Just a Little Better
By Matt Cohen
Published 2019 by Your Book Angel
Copyright © Matt Cohen

Printed in the United States

Edited by Keidi Keating

Layout by Christi Koehl

ISBN: 978-1-7335939-7-7

JUST A LITTLE BETTER

A leader's guide to becoming
"just a little better"
every day.

Greater success at work, at home,
and in your communities.

By Dr. Matt Cohen

INTRODUCTION

Just a little better. Hmm, what a powerful title you are thinking. Really swinging for the fences on this one. Granted, the title may a bit underwhelming but what I mean by "Just a Little Better" is the importance of progress. True success and a sense of accomplishment is not achieved in one amazing and sweeping act or transformation. Rather, sustained success, joy, and fulfillment are achieved when an individual is focused each day to become "just a little better." I hope you enjoy the following journey. It is designed in a way that will give some real-world examples and research supported ideas on how to be the leader you wish to be. Leadership is difficult and the very best of us face obstacles and challenges. As with all obstacles and challenges it is not only about overcoming them, but creating a habit, method or process that allows you to succeed over and over again. Whether you are a seasoned leader looking for a way to hone your skill, a leader who has come to a crossroads of potential burnout, or brand-new to leadership, this book is designed to help you immediately. I trust that you will take many of the suggestions and ideas to heart and that you will find them helpful as we all work toward becoming "just a little better."

ACKNOWLEDGEMENT

This book has been a journey over several years. I would like to acknowledge a few people. First on the list is my wife Tracy. She has been by my side throughout this process and has been a sounding board and motivator on countless occasions. I am blessed to have someone so far out of my league who is always willing to support and provide gentle encouragement.

My children, Matthew, Noah and Miles. You remind me that our stories continue long after we are gone and that each day really matters. I am proud to be your dad and I hope that when you are old men like me you will be good honorable men partly because of my love for each of you.

For my many team members I have worked with throughout the writing of this book who taught me so much about leadership and what it means to lead.

To my editor and publisher Keidi Keating who clearly put in a ton of effort in honing my writing so that it was more clear, concise and impactful. I know you cared about the work you were doing.

Lastly, I would be remise if I did not thank God. I know that he was working behind the scenes every time I sat down to write or thought about a concept to share. He reminded me the impact that creating something can have on the world.

Book Commitment

This book outlines three basic principles related to leadership in general. While I am not certain there will be earth-shattering breakthroughs, I do believe there are helpful reminders to you in your everyday leadership practices. I would also hope that by limiting it to three broad items you will be in a better position to build upon the ideas and build strength and structure into your version of the ideas I present. I say your version because in order to maximize any strengths and / or talents you must first remember that strengths and talents are unique to the person. The ideas I present here are meant to be used in a way that fits your style and capacity. Take them, build them, and make them yours.

AUTHOR BACKGROUND

I have wanted to write a book for many years. I have started many books and have somehow not had the wherewithal to continue to the end. It is indeed a commitment, and for the majority of my life I have felt relatively maxed out time-wise. Adding something that required the time and commitment of a book seemed practically impossible, and with each failed attempt that impossibility seemed even more certain. So, what is different now you ask? I have come to a point in my life where I have more peace, knowledge, and do not feel as overwhelmed. I am still busy, I still have a full plate in front of me each day, but my priorities and commitments have changed to the point where writing and then launching this book makes sense. Also, I have noticed a recent trend and demand for books that were a bit more brief and actionable. Knowing that even a slightly shorter book could be helpful and needed also helped to inspire me to begin the process.

The purpose of this book is to provide some thoughts, concepts, and methods on how to help you become the leader you have always wanted to be. It is also designed to help define proven methods and behaviors that can help a student of leadership better understand personal success and fulfillment. With that said, I am still on the journey as well. I have taken many missteps and have made enough mistakes to fill a book, but I have also found some success and methods to achieve that success built on a life of experience, academic study, and perspective. I believe each of us has been placed here for a purpose. That purpose is broad and unique to each of us but somehow the common denominator for all of us is to make the world better and to improve the lives of others. I hope and pray that the concepts and ideas within this book will help you to better fulfill your unique purpose.

I figure I would begin by telling you a bit about me, as this will help give you a perspective on where I am coming from while potentially being somewhat interesting. Here we go. You likely know this already as it would be somewhere on the outer portion of this book, (or I really need to work on my approach to book covers) but my name is Matt Cohen. I have a PhD in Leadership and have been interested in the dynamics of leaderships for the majority of my adult life. I grew up in two very distinct places. My first memories are from New Brunswick, New

Jersey. The neighborhood was nice and was made up of what seemed like thousands of townhomes made up in some type of masterplan community. Within my section of the neighborhood there were forty townhomes laid out in a square. In fact, I believe that is what the name of the development was: Dayton Square. It was awesome! Each row had ten or so townhomes and had at least three to six kids around my age, and across the whole square there may have been a total of 14 children living in the neighborhood and we were all close friends. We went to school together, we played together after school, and had sleep overs, and since the neighborhood was shaped the way it was, all the parents could keep an eye out for us as we played. My dad was a salesman for his father's company and my mom stayed at home to take care of me and my older sister. While there was no picket fence it was as perfect as I could have imagined. However, as with most things in life, it did not stay ideal for long.

I believe the first time my dad went on an extended "business trip" was when I was ten. I don't remember the exact timing but I do remember missing him tremendously. He would need to leave often and would always return with a small gift. The gift I recall the most was a GoBot. I do not remember the name of it but it was very similar to the Transformer Bumblebee and it was awesome, (well, as awesome as a knock off Transformer could be). Anyway, these trips became longer and longer and more frequent, and after about a year or so Mom and Dad told me that Dad was sick and that we (Mom and I) would need to start taking care of him. It was odd because as my dad was telling me this he seemed perfectly fine, however after only a few hours it was clear something was really wrong.

Later that day I found my dad looking a bit lost in the parking lot of the complex we lived in. I asked him what he was doing and he explained that he was trying to find his car, which was right in front of us. He then had difficulty remembering which townhome was ours. I cannot express in words how impactful that moment was, to see my brave, strong, former Marine dad, lost, scared, and confused, and needing his ten-year-old son to find the way home from a hundred yards away. It changed me. I am sitting on a plane right now with tears in my eyes as I realize this was the moment I understood the fragility of life and that I would never have the same dad again.

Mom and I were Dad's caretakers for the next four years or so. Many books have been written on the topic of Alzheimer's but if I can just emphasize it, it is a devastating disease. My father was diagnosed with early onset Alzheimer's when he was 54 years old. The "business trips" he had over the previous year were really trips to try to treat my dad. His Alzheimer's was accompanied by Parkinson's and from the age of ten until fourteen I watched my father slowly disappear mentally and physically. At the age of fourteen, my mom (who had recently been diagnosed with cancer) and I could no longer care for my father. He did not know who we were; in fact, he often confused us for demons or dragons and was scared of us, and could not walk without assistance. He moved into a full-time facility and died two years later as someone barely recognizable. I am sharing this portion of my life because the experience was devastating and life-shaping. I have looked at the world since then with a perspective that has helped to shape me into the person I am today. The loss of my wonderful, beautiful, and loving dad helped to shape me today.

Before I move on from my dad I wanted to share one nice story as well from my time with him that also taught me something. When I was seven or eight I would get terrible leg cramps. I would wake up in the middle of the night with excruciating pain and would nearly be in tears. My dad Elliot Cohen would wake up (after he had a long day of work) and bring me warm towels to place on my legs. He would then tell me stories to try to keep my mind off the pain, and he would do this multiple times throughout the night until the pain subsided. He would then still wake up early in the morning and head to work before I even awoke. These moments, the still of the night, just him and I. The compassion he expressed to help me, the stories, and the love... I mean it, love, compassion, empathy, warmth... all wrapped up in the hot compress of a towel on an aching leg, was beautiful. This memory and the generous soul of Dad is important to me and it is a constant reminder of the power of compassion and empathy toward others.

My mom, I would be remiss if I did not spend some time on her as well. This lady was no joke. She was powerful and brave and always put family first. She kept everything running, even as Dad got sicker and her cancer worsened. As all the money ran out due to medical expenses and the fact that my dad could no longer work, she made every effort to make sure we did not feel "without." We did our best, she made the best grilled cheese from that government cheese and was always there to give advice when I needed it. My mom would say something to the effect that, "while we may be "in need" we will never be needy." We will still do all that we can do for ourselves and will help others as best we can. Wow. I am pumped even remembering that right now. This lady had cancer, she had to take care of her husband, deal with the government in order to get the help we needed, but she still busted her butt to make sure my life and the lives of others were better. My mom was a rock, and passed to me the idea of "grit" and to do my best to consider others when making decisions and living my life.

When I was 19 or 20, shortly after I joined the military, I received a call from my older brother advising me to come home, as Mom was in the hospital and they were not sure how long she had left. I took the first flight out of Minot, ND to Charlotte, NC and made it to the hospital by late afternoon. I entered the room in which my mom was to find her nearly lifeless. I grabbed her hand and she looked up at me. It was almost like a switch flipped and she perked up slightly, and while she could not say much I could tell she was waiting for me. As if she would not let death come without seeing her baby boy one more time. You see, we were a team, her and I, for a long time. That day in the room she saw me in uniform (as I thought she would like that) and she knew that I would be okay. I held her for a very long time. She could not really speak but she was very verbal, and two hours later she left us.

The relationship with your parents is one of the most important relationships one can have. I was sixteen when my dad died and twenty when my mom passed and many years have passed since then but they are foundational to who I am. Their lives, our experience together, and their passing are segments of my life that were a true journey that played out with many emotions of both joy and sorrow, both reliant on the other. God was always with us, He is with us now, and their legacy and lessons live on in me and now also my children. This is a great reminder that our stories are not complete at the end of our lives, but rather the story continues through the lives of our children and their children. Your story is written in stone and can often be seen for generations. No matter the challenges we face, remember, through darkness light can come and through the light so lights the world.

Now back to partnering with you...

This book is meant to share some ideas and concepts that I have found to be successful so far in my career and life. It also encapsulates a substantial amount of learning as an adult learner and researcher who has completed a PhD within the field. I preface this by saying that I have made many mistakes. I still often struggle and I do not have all the answers. I have read hundreds of books on leadership and have found that the vast majority of them speak about not only what is successful but what is also risky and\or potentially failure points. What I hope is conveyed here is a few valuable points and inspirational concepts that allow the reader to understand that the struggle of leadership and balance in life is real and that those who are able to recognize the challenge and still persevere are the individuals who can achieve the most in life.

Who I am now...

Who am I to share my life experience with you? What is this guy all about you ask? Well, as I said, my name is Dr. Matthew Cohen (Matt) I am a Vice President of Customer Service for a Fortune 100 company, as well as a Professor of Leadership and Business at Southeastern University. I have been in leadership for more than twenty years and have experienced many highs and lows throughout my career. Through my experiences I have been able to examine and study what has helped. Often, it comes down to very basic items done regularly a little at a time with specific emphasis on three areas of our lives.

Chapter 1
AN OVERALL PERSPECTIVE

I try to look at life in separate compartments. However, each is connected. The first of which is a **spiritual** life. A core belief of balance and connection with a higher purpose, power and/or idea. I have a Christian perspective but I also understand that each person is different. The main idea in the spiritual balance section is to understand that we are here for a higher purpose and that what we do is not solely to meet the needs and wants of our individual self. We are here to fulfill a higher purpose. We have skills, talents, and gifts that are designed and meant for something. Do not waste them. I want to be clear here… to have a spiritual balance is not something that requires you to know specifically why you are here. It starts with knowing you are here for a reason. You should "*care that you are here,*" because it matters. You matter, and what you do matters. The sooner you can get out of your own head and realize that you are an important part of something far greater, the quicker your own self-imposed barriers are torn down, and the faster you will begin to achieve the type of success and joy you are looking for. It starts with a little bit of understanding.

One's purpose can be often associated with spirituality. Purpose as a Noun is the identification and understanding of an intent. However, having one is not enough. It also needs action as you seek your purpose and as you work on it you then begin to *live purposely*. You can often read about how to find purpose. *The Purpose Driven Life* by Rick Warren is a nice example and direction (Warren, 2003). In his work, Warren discusses three significant questions: Why am I alive? Does my life matter? And what on earth am I here for?" It leans into the idea of not only living for success and survival but real significance. This is a fantastic approach and one I use in my own life. In that vein I recently attended a sermon by Pastor Joe Champion of Celebration Church in Round Rock\Georgetown, TX where he shared his ideas of purpose, and I found his examples to be exceptional. In his sermon he states the following concepts and this is how I interpreted them:

➢ **Purpose: It will start when you start to serve.**

I truly like this idea and it resonates with me as it speaks to the importance of looking externally.

What are the needs of the world? This does not need to be some global purpose. This could be a simple need in your business, those you work with, and so on. Finding purpose can certainly be grand and magnificent. However, it can also be quiet and simple. Regardless of scope, start with serving others.

➤ Purpose: It really is not your purpose:

Okay, this is a big one. I realize not everyone reading this has a relationship with Christ. So, this may not seem fully baked. However, I love this one and many of my friends also thought this was a powerful statement. What this meant to us was that we are not here to fulfill what we want. Rather, we are here to somehow deliver the gifts, talents, and expectations of a supernatural intent. God wants us to do things, He has a plan and purpose for all of us, and He has given us all of the resources needed to fulfill that intent. For my non-Christian friends and readers, you may have an alternative source of a supernatural purpose, or you may not believe in some type of religious aspect to this. To you, I say this. A purpose not being your purpose may indicate that you are not here to fulfill some internal goal, dream, or accomplishment. This section may reference, to you, the idea that you are here as part of a bigger picture where your purpose may be tightly woven into a broader tapestry that may also assist friends, loved ones, even strangers you have not met yet. You are here as part of a "*Purpose Symphony*" where your purpose helps to fuel others and vice-versa.

➤ Purpose: Your purpose requires some unpacking:

What does this mean? I really had to pay attention to and think about this one. The idea around this one, at least how I interpreted this, was that you must really consider and "unpack" what it is that stirs you. Some questions that you might ask yourself during the unpacking...

- What do you think you might enjoy if you tried it?

- What is important to you?

- Are there others that you look up to and what about their lives impresses you the most?

- Are there opportunities within your current lifestyle that you could introduce small changes to that may align with your needs and desires?

- During your quiet moments of thought do you get a sense for what you should be doing?

The list goes on and on but my recommendation and what I try to do sometimes is think and write. Think about it and write it down. Go back to it and repeat. It takes time, it takes "unpacking." Heck, I am still searching so I use this method too. Maybe purpose changes overtime based on life situation, etc. So just don't unpack once and move on. Repeat every few years.

➢ **Purpose: Purpose requires purpose friendly relationships:**

This speaks to me in the way that it emphasizes the importance of others. Recently, I was at a work meeting where we were discussing the recent merger of two large business units. It was a great move for the company and we were all excited to have these additional team members. The leader of the new teams said something along the lines of, "He was bringing some real horsepower to the group." My response to him was, "Just make sure that horsepower is pushing in the right direction." Your relationships will either help you in your purposeful results or they can slow you down, so be careful.

➤ Purpose: Your purpose will make history:

Whether you want it to or not, what you accomplish in this world will have some type of influence on your personal history and potentially beyond. Your acts and actions have far reaching impact. Do the type of purposeful work that history will smile upon.

Purpose continued

You can get direction and purposeful thought from a host of sources. Recently, my three-year-old son Noah, asked me, "What is life?" Wow. that is one heavy question! I gave it some serious contemplation and began to expand about God and how He gives us each a spark called a Soul, and then I stopped for a moment to ask him what he thought life was. His response gave me goosebumps. He looked at me intently, crinkled his nose a little, and responded with, "Life is curiosity." I thought to myself, 'how in the world did he come up with that one?' He should be writing this book. Maybe he heard it on TV or something but... that was an awesome answer. I gave it some serious thought and realized that the happiest times of my life were fueled by some level of curiosity. Over the course of our lives, it seems that we often get to a point in our marriage, career, friendships, or hobbies where we know basically what we get. What we get could be great, but we are not surprised often anymore. You wake up around the same time, kiss your spouse, walk your dog, make breakfast, go to work, work, come home, kiss your spouse, walk the dog, eat dinner, go to bed. I realize I am oversimplifying and not everyone's life is as mundane as this, but I think you get the point. Even if each of those activities are epic, there are often very limited opportunities for surprise, thereby decreasing our level of curiosity. Now imagine the lens of a child where so much is still new, and nearly everything is an opportunity to be curious.

If we peel back a bit further on curiosity for a moment, we have to first think about what it means to be *successfully curious*. I add the adjective successfully because there is a difference between being curious about something potentially relevant and something potentially irrelevant. What is relevant and not relevant is not for me to decide, and it is very individual to the person. I just want to point out searching on Facebook aimlessly for the cutest puppy picture certainly is akin to curiosity but I warn that it lacks the potential of contributing to a person's success. *Successful curiosity* is the curiosity to do or learn something that has the potential to enhance someone's life. What are you curious about? What would you like to learn more of? I still struggle sometimes to come up with new things that really interest me, which can improve my life or the life of others around me, but I still try.

I would like to add that having an item of curiosity that can lead to something with a "start, a middle and an end" can make it that much more impactful. Often, I have found that the most successful people I have met have a track record of finishing things that at one point interested them. It is not that they never fail, but rather they fail regularly but still manage to finish. It is better to *finish and fail* than to never complete something. A lot of us stay stuck in "the middle" of something we are working on; we hope to finish, but we are not quite there yet. We often come up with reasons we are still "stuck in the middle." Yes, I am thinking of that song right now as well (good song by Stealer's Wheel" take a quick break and listen). We come up with "reasons" about why we have not finished yet and there are things that get in the way sometimes. However, often if I have not completed something, it is on me. I slacked off, lost interest or thought it was too difficult. If you can get out of the middle and complete things, especially the things you are curious about, you create a powerful emotion.

How often have you heard someone telling you about how they have been working on and off on something for years, and they sound almost defeated in the pursuit? Be *Victorious in the Pursuit,* making a bit of progress regularly. The completion of something even as small as a common task has similar characteristics emotionally to small victories (Brown & Lahey, 2015). In a study designed by Brown and Lahey to demonstrate the power of task completion with motivation, researchers found that even the simple task of entering data into a spreadsheet correctly, can have influence on the motivation to complete more. Of course, it is not always about simply completing more, but the momentum created by finishing something cannot be denied. Do something, get out of the middle.

One tip I have found is to try to determine what specifically is inhibiting completion and then creating a subtask within the larger task that may be able to get the machine moving again. For example, say you want to start your own consulting company. You have been talking about if for years and may have plenty of ideas. Great ideas are not enough and you are stuck in the middle. In order to get the motor running, what if you created one *small sub-subject* in this particular case… say it is one presentation rooted in your idea that you can begin to share with fellow employers or colleagues. This presentation can be the one sub-subject that you begin and then complete that can help to propel the larger idea forward. The worst-case scenario is that you created a helpful presentation for your audience, however the best case is that you might have developed a key component of the consulting practice.

Completing things and the sense of fulfillment allows for us to have a deeper connection to what moves us. What moves us connects us to purpose thereby strengthening our potential for greater spirituality. Spirituality is the first component of this three-prong approach to getting a little better, now let's move on to the next area. Physical balance…

The physical element

Physical balance is another area I believe is important. Now, do not get me wrong, I am not a hyper athlete. If you look at me, you would not be impressed with me in one way or another. However, I try to exercise regularly, I eat relatively healthy, and believe that it is important to have a competitive spirit involved some type of physical activity. I appreciate a gym that is designed and run in a way that with each morning there is some type of team-based activity that has individuals not only striving for personal growth and physical improvement but also builds in fun competition. However, I have also enjoyed working out early in the morning at my home or by going for a simple morning run. I golf when I can and appreciate the competition of sport. Again, my knowledge around physical training and nutrition is seriously limited but I have learned over the course of my life that many of my lowest points are periods of time when there was not a clear focus on the physical aspect of my life.

I also want to emphasize the importance of good restful sleep. Finding the right amount of rest and ensuring it is part of the physical plan is more important than the plan itself. The overall idea here, as I discuss physical balance, is that you should do your best to be healthy and fit. Of course, this is to the best of your ability. Each of us is different, but if possible, your physicality should be something that *helps to enhance* your life not one that *detracts* from the other areas of life. The word physical directly relates to the body. If I were to go even deeper I would say we should be more concerned with the physiological aspect, which is how our bodies work. By understanding how your physiology works we can then understand the importance of the physical advantages of a solid level of fitness. Also, some type of competitive outlet allows for healthy channeling of the spirit that is in each of us. We innately have an element of competitive spirit and often no matter the reward individuals are motivated by an opportunity to excel through competition (Ganz & Hassett, 2008). This same idea of competition and then actively pursuing some type of competition can lead to greater success not only during the actual activity of whatever competitive outlet is chosen but throughout someone's entire life (Ganz & Hassett, 2008). To me that is a pretty powerful idea. Competition, not comparison, mind you, can be quite valuable to one's success.

I digress to comparison

Since this is a book and not an article I am going to digress a bit since I brought up the idea of comparison. When I began writing this book I was unaware of the theory known as "social comparison theory." Social comparison can be defined as the "process of thinking about information about one or more other people in relation to self" (Wood, 1996). While I was not aware of the theory, it makes complete sense. It seems each of us has some level of innate comparison gene. We find ourselves trying to "keep up with the Jones'" to a certain degree. A certain level of this "comparison gene" I find to be helpful. You may strive to work on a skill or talent that someone you look up to has demonstrated. I recall a leader I had many years ago who could almost immediately connect with people. She displayed a very high level of emotional intelligence and I would often find myself trying to hone my interpersonal skills so they would be more closely comparative to hers. Over time I did improve but I would become frustrated when I did not measure up to the example she was setting.

However, as you can expect, often social comparison can have a negative effect that can influence your self-esteem and confidence. The rise in popularity of social media has heightened the impact of social comparison (White, Langer, Yariv, & Welch, 2006) and it can be quite debilitating. A recent study was conducted that measured the responses of adult men and women as it related to frequency of social comparison with emotions and behaviors. This study determined that frequent social comparisons were associated with a range of destructive emotions and behaviors, including those directed toward self. The most prevalent self-directed emotion was guilt and the most prevalent behavior was lying (White, Langer, Yariv, & Welch, 2006). Social media has helped to connect the world. I realize there are many benefits to this, however it has also created an environment where individuals are constantly walking around and trying to determine how they measure up. If I just take Facebook for a moment I often see the perfect picture, or the "Best spouse, kid, #job, #vacation." I wonder how often a person may be reading that same post and trying to determine how they compare to that person. Life is too short, and at the end of our life we will not get a trophy or certificate recognizing how we did compared to everyone else. Ultimately, if you must compare, compare yourself to how you were the previous day. How am I progressing toward a goal? Will I learn something today that helped to make me a more effective parent, spouse, teacher, employee? You are not successful based on how you compare to someone else. True success is the journey toward becoming the person you can be, if you invest in yourself. The "*can be comparison*" is far more effective at driving personal success than trying to compare against anyone else. All this comparison talk and how it affects your mind leads me to the next section of the book, so please keep reading.

Mental strength

Mental health is another area of life that I find is often not talked about but is vital to leadership. I have personally struggled with a certain level of depression in my life. In fact, as I write these words I am fighting the tug of depression. Not trying to bum you out, I am fine, but I use that understanding of my own mental health as a catalyst to write. I know that writing helps to keep my mind focused on externally helping others as opposed to any sense of depression or pain (and it works by the way, as I am in a better state of mind already). While depression has been a battle, through God's partnership I have never allowed it to grasp me fully. Keep your mind sharp through continuous active learning that requires you to use critical thinking, memorization, and a real emphasis on that which is new to you. I have tried to address this through my doctoral program as well as learning more and more about the idea of mindfulness and the study of meditation, plus introducing Kung Fu to my fitness and mental health regimen. This learning has been vital to me and my growth. The PhD specifically forced me to study in a way that I have not done for many years. This pushes your ability to focus and apply significant thought. The use of mindful practices and the peace that can be found in meditation helps to improve my mental state and spiritual state.

Meditation and mindfulness have not only been helpful in my life and mental state, but they have been proven to help combat depression (Brewer, 2010). It helps to address substance abuse challenges. I realize that this book does not scream "how to fight substance abuse" but in my experience I have definitely seen my fair share of individuals who could use a bit of help here. I have worked with many high-level executives and peers who demonstrated some degree of substance abuse. It may have not been blatant and did not appear to impact their work but self-medication was occurring. Often, it would present itself through drinking alcohol to an extreme far too often. This was common practice for many. Many leadership jobs can be stressful with long days and difficult pressures and it may seem that an alcoholic beverage can curb a bit of the stress. It may start with the occasional beer after work or the glass of wine before bed. In and by itself no big deal but it can begin to spiral. Stress at work can contribute to the happy hours going longer, the glass of wine with dinner expanding to several, and the business trip allowing for increased consumption of alcohol when away from the knowing eyes of family and loved ones.

This overconsumption often occurs when leaders state, "It helps to take my mind off the challenges or focus of the day." High performers are often so focused on achieving the next great task that they turn to a vice in order to derail their mind from the intense pursuit. I have personally seen many great men and women in high pressure roles succumb to self-medication and increased consumption. This can, of course, have a significant negative impact on health and family. There are alternatives, one of which is meditation and an increase to mindfulness, which has been proven to provide vast benefits (Dasa & Brendel, 2017), which can help not only effectiveness in life but the ability to better manage through difficult times or intensity where previously self-medication or depression would have taken hold.

Again, do not get me wrong, I am all for the occasional margarita and often find my own mind difficult to move from the pursuit of some abstract goal. With meditation, I have truly been able to improve the way my mind functions, which has allowed me to have better balance. This book is a great example of a goal that I have right in front of me, but it also seems so far away. Some nights I want nothing to do with this book and simply want to relax or play with my son. On those nights I feel a bit guilty for not writing and continuing to delay the process. This is both a curse and a blessing as it does drive me to write but I must continue to work on allowing myself to have the freedom to not have every goal worked on every day, making time for other areas of life.

Each of us is surrounded by opportunities to make progress on countless goals. As a leader you are not only responsible for you own goals but also the progress of others. For me personally it was difficult to follow my own advice around freeing up my own mind in order to pursue all areas of my life. I found that by improving my commitment to meditation my ability to not only focus on my own goals but the results of others was bolstered.

In one particular study I conducted, around team management, I concluded that mindful leaders have an improved ability to react to performance degradation and addressing behavior issues within the workplace

(Cohen, 2016). This improvement allows the leader to more effectively focus their attention across the board as opposed to one or two specific individuals or tasks. Mindfulness can also help to increase mental effectiveness and awareness. A heightened awareness may help an individual recognize when there are indications, while sometimes subtle, that may need to be dealt with or acknowledged. Recognizing a slight uptick in tension, anxiety or stress may allow the more mindful person to take a deep breath, walk away, or acknowledge appropriately in order to move past it before it (for lack of a better phrase) "pops."

Leaders who build meditation into their lives are able to better control unhealthy mental pursuits and have been shown to increase the chemicals in the brain needed to sustain a mental balance. This ability to mitigate depression and potential self-medicating may be specifically related to the increase to brain function. This increase in brain function has been supported by countless research activities and indicates that an enhancement to brain function gives a greater ability to conduct deep thought processes and make decisions more effectively (Nonprofit World, 2015).

The three areas of focus (Physical, Mental, and Spiritual) have inherent benefits that have been and will continue to be discussed throughout this book. One particular benefit that I would like to point out is that they each enhance resilience. Whether it is building physical resilience, mental resilience or spiritual resilience, the more you have the better you will be when facing difficulties. The ability to face and deal with difficulties is what I have found to be the biggest differentiator when it comes to practical and successful leadership. Individuals who demonstrate a strength of resilience demonstrate an enhanced ability to cope and compete (Kuntz, Malinen, & Naswall, 2017).

Resilience matters, and it can only be created through the type of work and dedication that can seem difficult. The most powerful type of resilience is what I like to refer to as *Radical Resilience*; the belief that building strength in a controlled environment can lead to radical real-world resilience. Going to the gym, spending quality time in scripture, or in the development of mindful practice through meditation allows you to achieve when the environment is not as controlled: Work, office, community, family, and the list goes on. Resilience is often described as the capacity of an individual to withstand hardship, and while facing adversity continue to lead a functional and healthy life (Turner, 2001). In my experience, a leader who tries to develop resilience not only is better able to deal with obstacles that are difficult, they are often able to take something that appears to be difficult, and make it look relatively painless. Here is what I mean...

When I was learning how to drive, one of the most difficult parts was using a stick shift. Between all of the gears and the combination of the clutch and determining the right rpms to shift at, I was constantly confused. I recall vividly grinding gears, shifting too early, and going like 25 miles per hour in fifth gear and stalling out. A complete mess would be my summation of my manual driving skills. I would often put off learning because I dreaded my constant failure. I dreaded the looks at the stop sign with an intersection with a slight decline and how often I would stall out my car and nearly back in to the person behind me. I would proudly exclaim, "I will just drive an automatic" so that I would not need to deal with the problems. Bottom line, I did not like to drive a manual because I did it poorly. There was a clear option other than a manual transmission so why waste my time? Simple, right? Let's just move on to a car that I can drive easier. This is an example of a lack of resilience and perseverance. This, of course, is a very basic example. Now here is where resilience kicks in. I continued to practice, and I continued to stall the car, but less. I continued to grind the gears, but less. After sometime, I became proficient. I would even venture to say that I became relatively good at driving stick shift. In fact, I surmised that I got to the point where my resilience paid off and moving through the gears became an activity that was easy. The vast majority of the actual shifting of the car was handled at a subconscious level. What was once difficult, daunting, and frustrating was now offloaded to the subconscious.

As I said, this is a basic example but speaks clearly to the fact that if we do not persevere we will likely never get to the point where we can truly excel. Whether it be driving a car or giving difficult feedback to a challenging employee, it is all about persevering, being resilient and committed until proficiency begins to manifest itself.

Chapter 2
SPIRITUAL STRENGTH

Spiritual strength... wow, that sounds very weighty! I suppose it could be but it is really simple in my mind. At the most basic level it means having some level of peace in one's life. We live in a world, especially as leaders, where the volume of worldly activity is overwhelming. We are expected to respond to emails nearly immediately. "Hey, did you see that email I sent to you two minutes ago?" We have expectations at home, at church, family, personal commitments, and responsibilities at work. We are not designed to process this much activity without help.

In his book, *The Organized Mind,* Daniel Levitin explains exceptionally well how the volume of assault on our busy brains is greater than it has ever been and many leaders try to offset the activity through multi-tasking (Levitin, 2014). The problem is that our conscious mind only can process about forty bits of information per second. This is not a lot of processing power at the conscious level. However, the entire brain to include the subconscious can process data at a staggering 3.5 quadrillion bytes 2.2 billion megaflops at 20 watts (Fischetti, 2011). As a point of reference, in the event you don't know what a megaflop is, which I did not, an iPad 2 can process data at 64 billion bytes and 170 megaflops, which is far slower than the human mind. You can see that the potential of the mind is quite outstanding. As of some very recent measurements, the only computer that can process information faster than our brain is the K computer, Fujitsu, that can process 30 quadrillion bytes or 8.2 billion megaflops. However, it requires 9.9 million watts of power (about 10,000 homes worth of electricity) as compared to our brain only requiring 20 watts (Fischetti, 2011).

In basic terms, our brain is still one of the most efficient processors of information of all time even when compared to super computers. The subconscious is working all the time and is ten times more powerful than the conscious mind. It operates during sleep in the form of dreams and it can be counted on to manage many of the most complex human tasks. Its processing power and the idea of speed and energy is an important aspect of the cognitive load theory that was introduced in the late 1980s but increasingly supported through neuroimaging research (Oakley, 2017). This theory correlates to our minds processing power.

A basic example is the process of tying shoes. I am

sure you can recall your childhood when tying shoes required substantial concentration and thought. It required the utilization of your working memory. Now, however, as an adult, the process of tying shoes is handled mainly via the subconscious. The more often you can download processes and procedures to your subconscious, the more capacity you will have within your working memory. Increased capacity in the working memory allows you to be more present in the now.

There is a lot of information above, so allow me to simplify. *You must offload before you can reload.* If you want to do more consciously you must create room and additional capacity. The best way to do that is to increase your working memory and offload some of your most mundane activity to your subconscious. I have chosen to discuss this here within the spiritual section because of the benefits of increasing working memory capacity through meditation. When you increase working memory capacity, or what some would call short-term memory, you are often more capable of what appears to be multi-tasking. However, this is not actually multitasking; it is the capacity to be a more agile thinker who is able to move from one focus to another quickly and more seamlessly.

I have met very few leaders who have really nailed

this one. I have, however, run across a couple that seemed to understand the idea of shifting quickly. In my opinion it is based on two items. The first is directly related to very obvious strength of mind and very good short-term memory. I would see leaders attend meetings and be able to recall minute details on a subject that is being discussed and correlate it flawlessly with previously completed items. You ask them to study some data and they can retain it very well, real signs of strong short-term memory. The other item that can also be correlated to is the amount of energy they expend on minor items. They very seldom get upset or seemingly distraught by things. The even keel they display may help to eliminate wasted energy and thought. This energy and thought could be related to anxiety, worry, anger, dread or any other possible emotions that saps the energy. Sapped energy equates to reduced capacity (Fine, 2017). There is no such thing as being an effective multitasker. There are those of us who can move quickly between activities but trying to multi-task is a futile effort and leads to worse recall and recognition (Angell, Gorton, Sauer, Bottomley, & White, 2016).

As I write this section, especially around the idea of trying to avoid multi-tasking, I am reminded of how difficult this is. I still fight the futile attempts to multi-task. More often than not I start to attempt to multi-task when my brain starts to wander a bit or even worse, get bored with the subject I am focused on. One thing leads to another and before I know it I have completely lost my train of thought on the first subject I was working in. I then try to regain control of what I was working in the first place only to lose track of the new thing I was working on and then it repeats itself until I basically stop both and drink some coffee… Not a good cycle, and one I still jump on, however now with less regularity.

When I think of an easy way to remind myself, I say something to the effect of, *"To try to multitask is likely trying to ride two bicycles at the same time; it is nearly impossible and does not get you to where you are going any faster. In fact, likely you wind up falling."*

Positively positive

Positivity has a positive (see what I just did there) effect on our performance and has elements of spiritual development. In the book the *Happiness Advantage,* Shawn Anchor suggests several methods of increasing happiness: Meditate, find something to look forward to, commit conscious acts of kindness, infuse positivity into your surroundings, exercise, spend money (but not on stuff), exercise a signature strength (Achor, 2010).

I knew a guy once who planned two vacations a year. Nothing major just time away from work with family and/or friends where he could enjoy himself and recharge. He would place them on his calendar at six-month intervals and he would look forward to them. He would be careful not to set them up as too grandiose in order to avoid a letdown but he always seemed to be looking forward to the next vacation. I caution a bit here because I have also seen teammates get into vacation mode way too early, but I think for the most part it is nice for people to have something to look forward to.

Having something to look forward to gives you something to think about during the rough days at work. If you have a family it gives you something to collectively talk about and prepare for. This preparation (even when it's just a vacation) helps to build teamwork. I, like you, may not always see my family as a team that I have to strengthen our teamwork skills but your *home team is one of the most important* teams you have. Why not treat a vacation getaway as a fun project you can plan for and then have play out? I love a project that results in something I enjoy and I certainly enjoy time away with family and or friends.

Looking forward to time away from the office for a vacation is one thing, but it can also be tremendously valuable to look forward to things on a daily basis. Potentially a good lunch with co-workers, a project that is near completion that will have significant results. A report that is utilized every day that highlights areas of improvement. Something I like to say is, *"Looking forward makes you keep your head up."*

When I think about what I look forward to the most at work it is often tied to a signature strength. Try to make your job the job you actually want instead of trying to find something else. I recall earlier in my career becoming so frustrated with my work and the potentially mundane activity that I would spend more time looking for another job than actually doing the job I did have. Has this ever happened to you? It was not until much later in my career that I realized I could enhance my current job by introducing work and activities I really enjoyed. For example, I really enjoy training people on new topics. I like the classroom environment and I am excited when I start to see people "get it." With that in mind I attempted to introduce a formal training into my work by once a month providing the staff a full-service training for my teams on a subject they expressed interest in. The event was not the only interesting aspect; the creation of the content also provided something to look forward to. These trainings added value to my team and they allowed me to express my training interests while still keeping in line with the goals of the company and my workforce. A complete win-win.

Another of my favorite quotes is, *"It is easier to make what you do what you love than to find something new to love."* I realize that this is not always possible and there are certainly examples in my life where my role simply could not work out for me, however I encourage you to attempt to examine your current roles and enhance them as opposed to moving on. In either case, find the positivity in your situation, as it is almost always there. Keeping your head up can help to propel momentum and progress. Don't let up and know the value of anticipation.

Deeper spirituality

Having a level of spirituality can mean quite a lot to some of us. It also has the potential to mean something very different to different people. I will try to define it as I use it and from there you can build your own version of its definition.

To me, for the purpose of my life, spirituality has to do with my true self. I believe that I am not the summation of my thoughts and experience but rather an internal self that I feel is my spirit. This spirit also allows me to find peace during times of stress and turmoil or direction when I feel as if I am uncertain of the direct path.

Of course, this understanding of my spirituality and the implementation of "being spiritual" are two different things. I remind you I am on this journey with you. I have not arrived necessarily nor am I certain you ever actually arrive but that does not mean we do not learn and teach while still on the path. Reminding myself each day that I am not my mind, my mind is simply a tool for my soul that helps to keep me... well, spiritual.

Within spirituality I find one level that deals with my faith in God. This is grounding, guiding, and loving. My connection to God has helped to make me the person I want to be. It has allowed me to find the path towards a greater relationship with Jesus. This relationship is the most important one in my life. It also helps to teach me a better way of being engaged in a relationship. With my wife, children, friends, co-workers no matter the setting strengthening my bond toward Christ is very similar to how one would strengthen a relationship with another person. In my own faith I find it to be a gift that God provided Jesus to be our conduit to our faith. Jesus wants that relationship and he is always reaching out; this is the same way we should be toward him and others around us. I have found that this desire for connection is often a core element beyond Christianity and serves many different faiths in a meaningful way.

Seek to be the strength of a relationship... do not rely on the other people to sustain it or make it better. This idea is most apparent with friends and family but it also goes beyond our close relationships. I like to think of relationships broadly and I once heard about the idea of the social contract. We each have a social contract with everyone we come into contact with. A social contract as I reflect on it means "you should not negatively influence anyone that you meet, run into, drive by, purchase something from, everyone and anyone." That means that you treat *all* others with a certain degree of kindness. If your day is going bad do not bring that negativity into anyone else's day. This can be hard as we are all human and not everyone demonstrates this same social contract, but it is there.

I use the *big sigh* example. I sometimes fall into the *big sigh guy* zone. You know the person who, when they walk by you or you ask them to do something, they let out that siggghhhh before they take action or move by. Does that sigh not take a little bit of wind out of the room? It is not fair to those around me when I do that. While it may not be intended it almost certainly has a negative influence on other people. Again, some days just are not as good as other ones. This is not an all or nothing kind of thing but know that your influence goes a long way so avoid the negative.

Contribute to the greater good

Positivity is a big deal but even beyond the positivity is the *power to contribute*. Always look for ways to add value to the lives of others. This does not have to be through grand acts. It can be simple. Maybe you see someone has listed a role or opening at their firm on LinkedIn. Old me says "not anything I'm interested in" and I move on quickly. New me, more often than not, at least takes a moment to consider "do I know someone who may be interested and might have the experience to do well in the role?" Or even further removed, do I know someone who may know someone who may be good for it? If I can think of someone I reach out with an email to make them aware. I also let the person who originated the talent researching post know that I will reach out to a few folks in my network to see if there is someone. Sometimes it works out and there is a connection, sometimes there are not. The key here is that I tried to be a connector.

Connecting people who can help one another is a tremendous value to the world. Be someone who connects and help others see the "*power of connection.*" Additionally, it improves your brand and people will see you as someone who enhances their network as opposed to just existing in it. We often hear people talk about building our network, or networking. The most important aspect of any network is the connection. Be a *conduit of that connection.*

Higher purpose

I hear the words "higher purpose" relatively often. I have likely said those words quite often as well. "What is my higher purpose?" "What am I here for?" "What is God's plan for me?" Likely, many of you have also heard or said these same words. I bring up purpose again because it relates to a "higher purpose." "Higher purpose" is linked to the spirituality area because, to me, this higher purpose we are often searching for is similar to spirituality because it deals with the connection to one's self, to one's purpose, this higher calling. A higher purpose is something I have searched for most of my adult life. If I could only find the higher purpose then I would be happy, successful, fulfilled somehow. I just have to figure out what that is. This was my mindset when I was frustrated with work. Or if my personal life was not going well I would blame it on me not being in a role that was fulfilling my "higher" purpose.

Here is the thing about finding your higher purpose. The mere fact that you understand there is one, is half the battle. Tell yourself right now that no matter what you are doing, you are indeed part of a higher purpose. You simply being you has tremendous value and you are, in fact, part of a higher purpose already. Once you realize this it helps to provide greater perspective on the everyday tasks you perform. Everything you do has value and nothing should be wasted. I once heard a great singer say to a struggling artist on one of those singing competition game shows, "Every word in a song matters; sing each of them with that in mind." This resonated with me in a very metaphysical way. Imagine how empowering it would be to imagine your life as a song, and that each day and moment were important notes, lyrics, and harmonies of that song. With this in mind sing them each with an understanding that your voice and efforts are part of something much larger than the individual note and have the potential to contribute to beautiful song.

I have recently found that there is power in helping to find your company's higher purpose. Companies have a certain level or responsibility to the areas in which they conduct business. In fact, research has indicated that 80% of the general public expect companies to not only increase profits but improve economic and social conditions in local communities (Stubbs, 2017). Whether it is a company doing good in the community or having a product or service directly related to improving a community, society, etc., there is always some meaning in the work. This meaning is not only inherently "good;" it can increase the attractiveness of the organization to its employees. Employees want to feel part of something that is adding value to the world and aware of its influence (Goler, Gale, Harrington, & Grant, 2018). This can go a long way in improving employee retention and engagement. Adding value and understanding that you are part of that value helps connect each of us to that higher purpose.

Know yourself... your true self

Who are you? Have you ever looked in the mirror and asked yourself that question? Many of us don't really know who we are. When meeting someone new we typically just roll off our name, maybe what we do for a living, where we are from, whose parents we are, and so on. Pretty bland answers most of the time. I still ask myself that same question quite often and I must admit I am still searching. I am closer to understanding who I am today than I was yesterday and likely tomorrow I will be even closer.

Knowing oneself begins with knowing that your true self really lies within. It is in there. Similar to that higher purpose conversation we just had. There is a you, inside of you (I know that sounds redundant but allow me a little artistic license). We often associate who we are with our life experience, our thoughts, our emotions, our education, and the list goes on. To some degree all of that is correct. Earlier in my life I would say much of who I was, was wrapped up inside of my mind. Basically, my mind was guiding the ship. Still today, I often find the mind is in charge, but here is the thing that is the real truth of who you are. Within each of us is a potential for spirituality that helps to fuel our healing, our ability to cope, and ultimately find meaning in our life (Uwland-Sikkema, Visser, Westerhof, & Garssen, 2018). Our brains, on the other hand, are simply another tool that we have in our arsenal to help us in our lives to be who we are, and do what we do. Knowing that the brain is simply a tool helps to make sure we stick to developing ourselves not just our knowledge.

Point of view

Recently, on one of my favorite podcasts, The James Altucher show, James was interviewing Sebastian Maniscalco, who is a relatively famous stand-up comedian recently mentioned in Forbes as making over 50 million dollars a year. The conversation led to how he became so good on stage. Sebastian talked about finding out who he really was and then being that person on stage and in life. His thought was that he could find that true person by gaining confidence in what he was doing. Once he gained confidence he found his point of view on life, and vice versa (Maniscalco, 2018).

He had an ability to understand how he interpreted the world, and this point of view allowed him to improve his ability to perform, connect with the audience, and improve his comedic prowess.

This resonated with me as I considered the ideas of confidence and point of view or perspective. Often, the confidence aspect is gained through experience, however you can more easily find a point of view. A point of view should align with what you believe in. What perspective on life do you use when working with employees, speaking to your spouse, guiding your kids?

"Your external interactions signify your internal truth." Finding my "internal truth" and differentiating what is in mind and what is in my soul, is best found through meditation and quiet reflection. Only with that connection can you truly be the person you were meant to be and lead others with a robust confidence that someone who is comfortable knowing themselves displays.

Knowing who you are helps to allow you to demonstrate that to others. If you do not know who you are how in the world will those who follow you know? This knowledge allows you to be genuine and being genuine helps when trying to connect with people and when building relationships. I think sometimes a leader tries to be something they are not in order to try to be what they expect their employees, peers or colleagues expect from them. When they cannot maintain "the act" they let people down and disrupt trust.

Often, if they were simply more genuine, meaning they are who they are, they might have avoided the let down or in the worst-case scenario, the appearance of betrayal or lies. Once someone feels misled or lied to it is difficult to ever regain trust. Without trust you will likely never truly get someone to work for and with you in a successful manner. The relationship between leader and follower is built on "trust and credibility." I like to say for your relationship *to be incredible, you must first be credible.* Allow your team to get to know what you are about and how you view the world.

If I peel this back a bit more I am reminded of a good story I recently heard from renowned author and speaker, Simon Sinek, who wrote the bestseller, "*It Starts with Why.*" He was discussing perspective on getting what you want and how to deal with situations. How you deal with situations can be a keen insight to your true self and how you operate.

In his story, he describes a time he and a friend were just finishing a run. It was an official race where when you arrive at the finish line you are met with many vendors providing waters, bananas, nutrition bars, and the like. One of the most popular vendors was at a table giving out free bagels. It was the longest line, but heck bagels are awesome so it totally makes sense. When Simon motioned to his friend to go grab one his friend said, "Are you kidding me? Have you seen that line? No way." What his friend saw was an incredibly long line, while all Simon saw was FREE BAGELS.

This speaks to the idea of knowing yourself well enough to know what you want and visualizing getting to it as opposed to the obstacle (like a long line) between you and that desire. There was a secondary element Simon discussed in this story. He explained that the line was created in a way where if you didn't mind reaching in and grabbing a random bagel you would not need to wait as long. The silent understanding was as long as you did not cut in front of anyone or impede anyone else in their pursuit they would not mind you reaching in. Simon gave up some of his choice when selecting the bagel but bypassed the longest parts of the line.

The lesson here is to prioritize what you really

want and weigh out the effort versus the reward. If you know you love nearly all bagels and are willing to enjoy whatever you blindly grab then reach away and avoid some of the wait. The only real requirement is, do not impede others as you find creative ways to reach your goals. I like this story as a great narrative of the power of perspective. How many times have you focused too much on the length of the line as opposed to that delicious bagel?

A personal story on perspective

Perspective can be both broad and extremely focused. Whether you are looking for a free bagel after a race or something much more substantial, perspective is a big deal. *"Perspective is paramount."* A lot matters in this world. Much of our time is spent trying to determine what it is that "matters." Projects at work matter. How you treat your neighbors matters. The time you spend with family matters. We walk around every day assigning a score to nearly everything we do to the "matters meter." Taking out the trash, well that matters, give it a two. Walking the dog, maybe that is a three. Kissing your wife goodbye, a six? Getting that project in on time at work, that is a ten for sure, or is it? Then there are contextual items on the "matter meter." How do people view me as a leader, father, husband, employee, co-worker? Am I living up to expectations? Are the expectations high enough?

This book is being written over the course of some time. I am not in an office somewhere knocking this out in a month or so, but rather over a period of time. I have completed this book as time allowed and have been able to grow throughout the process. Because of this length of time I have learned more as I have written and I like to try to add lessons as I go along. This lesson relates to the "matters meter."

I just had my third child this week. His name is Miles Elliott Cohen. He is the culmination and a gift from God after a long journey of trying to conceive him. It took about two years but he arrived a few days ago. As I write this portion of the book I am sitting on a smallish loveseat in our bedroom leaning up against one of the mega-pillows my wife used to sleep during her pregnancy. It's like a 7 ft long U-shaped pillow and I have barely any room to sit, but I am comfortable none the less. I am in the dark as Miles has finally fallen asleep after many hours of trying to get him comfortable enough to do so. I am sitting here on watch to ensure he does not have trouble breathing or roll off the bed where he fell asleep. Yes, I know he should be in his own bed with no blankets or pillows on his back, etc., however this is where he fell asleep so we will take it. I serve as the "sleep sentry" watching Miles sleep while I hear the familiar sounds of my wife and her breast pump resonating from the living room as my three-year-old runs around saying, "When is Daddy going to be done?"

It is difficult for me to just sit there. Even as sleep sentry I needed to do something, so I picked up my laptop and began doing some work. Approving some expense reports, preparing the team for a site visit next week, taking a look at a couple spreadsheets I was not able to see earlier in the week. Once I finished, I looked at Miles sleeping and was inspired to add some content to this book about what really matters.

So now we go back in time a bit... a few weeks previously the OBGYN for my wife, stated, "Oh yeah he is ready to come. It could be any day." With that piece of information, I sent out a coverage plan for my business unit, notified everyone who my out of office contacts would be, and started the plan that my team and I had developed for my time away. Everyone was ready to go, my boss was appreciative of my preparedness, and I felt good that based on the doctor's comment some time over the next three to five days baby Miles would arrive. We were ready and excited!

Two weeks had passed and he had still not arrived, and I felt inpatient. I had prepped everyone at work, built a great plan, and now felt like I was creating undue stress on my work team. Additionally, we had arranged for my wife's mom to visit so that we would have someone here in the event we needed to go quickly in the middle of the night. With Grammy here we could leave our three-year-old at the house without having to contact neighbors or friends nearby. It was a plan, a process, and I like to stick to plans.

"Why is this taking so long? I have a lot going on at work. Why can we not move this baby having thing along?" Crazy, right? I was trying to rush God and Miles to match my timetable. The birth of a child was not happening on my schedule and I was inconvenienced. I know, it is ridiculous. My wife was also ready, as I am sure most pregnant woman are toward the end of pregnancy.

After our last regularly scheduled doctor's appointment it was recommended that the baby was more than full term, so just go ahead and induce. A lot of parents induce, and some doctors believe 39 weeks is the best time to induce labor (Marguilies, 2016). So, my wife and I considered it, thought about how much easier it would be to schedule it from a planning perspective, and agreed to schedule it for a Monday morning. Mom-in-law was at home watching the three-year-old, my work plan was a bit later but now in place, and we happily went to the hospital to deliver our sweet little baby boy.

We arrived at our hospital room and began the process of induction, breaking the water, adding the Oxytocin, which is the medicine delivered intravenously in order to prompt delivery. Contractions began, and we were on our way. However, our son was not ready, and would not get in the correct position for delivery. After several hours of pushing and the OBGYN trying to physically reposition our child's head through what appeared to be a painful and difficult manual manipulation, he would not move the way we needed and he was showing signs of stress as my wife's tailbone pressed upon his tiny forehead.

As more doctors entered the room, including a trauma professional and the on-call pediatrician, we had to decide between a C-section immediately or attempt one more natural method with the additional use of forceps (something we have read terrible stories about). Our OBGYN explained she had been trained in how to use forceps and wanted to try before moving to a C-section. We agreed and after a few moments of pushing and navigating with the forceps, our son arrived. He emerged, gave his first cry, and was given to Momma, but only for a brief moment as he quickly showed signs of tremendous breathing challenges.

The pediatrician immediately brought Miles to the trauma area where the room was set to work on him. His breathing was extremely labored and could not be maintained on his own without ventilation. The doctor advised us he appeared to have underdeveloped lungs. They connected him to a respirator and I watched this tiny little human fight for his next breath, observing his entire body heave in order to give every ounce of his strength to the acquisition of one more breath. I have never gotten down on my knees in public prayer beyond the confines of my church but there I was finding a small corner in the room where I could speak to God. I apologized for rushing Him, and asked for healing for Miles and to guide the hands and hearts of everyone involved in trying to get Miles to a stable place. After my prayer I found it very important to not only be in the room with Miles but to physically connect with him. There were several hospital personnel all around him as they poked and prodded my little boy but I found a space on his right side. I knelt down beside him and took his little hand. He immediately gripped my index finger and looked in my direction. His chest still heaved and the sound of the respirator filled the little space. It was the "busiest stillness" I had ever felt. Many people, many machines, a lot of noise, but within that little space where my eyes met his and our hands held each other there was a connection and stillness. I could tell my presence eased him and my presence was the third one in that little space. It was me, Miles, and the Spirit of God.

I felt compelled to sing softly to Miles and he listened. I know like 38% of a thousand songs so I make up a lot of words but he seemed to like my made-up versions of "I Can Only Imagine," "Stand by Me," and "Lean on Me," and several others that were more made up than accurate. As I sang softly, and Miles and I connected, his breathing became slightly less labored. He seemed to be finding the strength, easing his efforts. Within about 20 minutes, his respirations had reached the normal levels per minute. As tests continued on Miles, the next obstacle was his blood pressure, which had taken a turn toward the worse and it was time for the doctors to re-engage their efforts and I was asked to leave the room. I could tell by their faces that things were not going well. I left the room after ensuring that each of the healthcare professionals in the room knew we were counting on them.

I returned to my wife who had been anxiously awaiting my return and an update on baby Miles. She herself was still being worked on by the OBGYN after a difficult delivery. I let her know that Miles' breathing was improving and they were going to continue to work on him and run tests. They worked on Miles for the next two hours. I continuously checked in. They explained that if he did not improve he and I would need to go to the nearest Prenatal Intensive Care hospital. As the time passed, I sent texts to many friends asking for prayers to kick in big time. My wife and I comforted each other as we waited for an update to tell us all was well with our baby boy. At last they returned to give us an update... and this time it was with Miles. He had improved enough to return to Momma.

I share this personal story to give you an insight on how my perspective changed. In this particular case we were blessed and God was engaged throughout the process and helped us through what felt like a scary and painful few hours. The impatience I once felt was such a distant memory. The feeling about how my work would be effected by a delayed delivery date was meaningless. Ultimately, in contrast to the wonderful arrival of baby Miles, none of it really mattered. My perspective was distorted and my impatience and inconvenience was a juvenile reaction and state of mind. My perspective now looks to find what is truly important as opposed to what may seem important in the moment. Learning to know the difference takes time but is a valuable tool for life.

This life event was impactful, but I also realize many of you have had tremendously daunting events take place in your life. I trust that each of you has likely already learned this lesson albeit a powerful and painful one. If reading this has stirred any pain inside of you, I apologize, and please know that you are still loved and cherished. Regardless of individual life experiences the lesson here is still clear. Family, life, and love all take precedent. Act in life in a way that treasures and protects those three things. Do not try to rush them or put them on a timetable. You must allow some things to move at their own course. Pay attention to what you need to do in the other aspects of life but know that at the end of the day, your year, your life, it will be family, the life you lived, and the love you shared that will define you most significantly.

Power of love

Since I am on the subject of love as I type out that header I think of Huey Lewis's tune, "That's the Power of Love," from one of the Back to the Future films. An awesome song in my humble opinion and technology is so amazing. I write power of love, I think Huey Lewis, I punch it in my phone, and now I am watching a video on my phone of a music video with clips from Back to the Future. Crazy, right?! Alright, back to what power of love means to success and leadership. I realize love is a fairly straight forward idea but, to me, love is both a noun and a verb. Meaning, love is a feeling, it is God, it is what someone feels for another person, their community, their faith, their family, and others in the world. Love as a verb, as in *to show love,* is the actual manifestation of the noun love into action. To care for others, to put the needs of others above your own, to contribute to the world in a way that makes the lives of others better.

The idea of love in leadership is not a new one (Biro, 2014). In order to practice love, you should surround yourself with people to love. In your community potentially find a group in your church that shares a common interest. A small group atmosphere in the community church helped me to be grounded. The bonds within this group should have nothing to do with social status, jobs, or worldly focus. There are many groups beyond the church you can join. The goal is to potentially find a place or group of others who share some type of interest or hobby where you can collectively care for each other, and in some cases hold each other accountable for actions.

Do acts of love; for family, community, your country, a charity… the "what" is not the priority, just find something close to your heart and show love. Volunteer, help others in need, spend time with someone that values your input. Whether grand or small, potential acts of love are always possible. Love can often be confused with a word that is weak, especially in leadership. People can confuse love, and the empathy associated with it, with leadership that allows things to transpire or "slide" without ramification. Love is not a weakness; in fact, to truly love others can be quite difficult and requires personal discipline and dedication. The reason it can be so difficult is because many times those you are trying to love do not reciprocate. We must sometimes show those who show us the least love, the most love and grace. I would not necessarily go around seeking the most difficult people in the world but when you encounter them stand your ground and be the type of person and leader who can still show grace during challenging circumstances. Many people in the world require a lot of grace, so be an abundant *grace giver.*

As I stated before, surrounding yourself with people who show love can also be beneficial. I often find the simple act of eating a meal with someone who cares for me beyond my immediate family can be tremendously beneficial. I think one of the reasons is that they help you keep your mind off the most pressing of things. You can have simple talks about movies, vacations, what is going on with family, and so on. This is a good way to spend your energy in the company of others doing nothing of much value other than spending time together.

Surrounding yourself with those who love and honor you also helps to show you how to act toward others. Many of the most successful people I know ensure they spend time investing in meaningful relationships and ensure family and friends are part of their life on a regular basis. I am often reminded of the story of Moses in Exodus 17 during the

Israelite battle with Amalek. The Amalekites were savage warriors and it required God's intervention to help the Israelites to defeat them. He provided this support via Moses who observed the battle from the top of a hill with his brother Aaron and his friend Hur. Whenever Moses raised his hands, the Israelites would begin to win and take more ground, and when he tired and lowered his hands the Amalekites would begin to gain ground. After much time had passed, Moses became too fatigued to stand, so he sat on a stone, but as time progressed his arms still began to tire and fall to his sides. At that moment his friend Hur and his brother Aaron stood at Moses's side to hold his arms up for him. In time, the Israelites defeated the powerful King Amalek and his army. When I think about this story I am certain that God did not need Moses to hold his hands up, as he could have acted without Moses. However, to me, it spoke to the idea that God wants us to rely on others and have the types of relationship where we can count on people, even though He has already given us the gifts we need. We are all connected, so make the connections mean something.

I do want to caution that love does not typically find you. You find it. However, you must sometimes be patient. Often, we give up on potentially great possibilities that we would find incredibly rewarding because we lack patience. I think this is partly related to the changes in society because we no longer have to wait for much. We can receive feedback almost immediately on social media. We can google or ask Alexa to answer nearly every question we have. So when we look for meaningful work or relationships or the ability to make an impact we expect it to arrive as quickly as our delivery order from grubhub. Love, meaningful contact, making a significant contribution, are all things that take time and effort. Do not become frustrated to the point where you give up before you legitimately give the time and effort needed.

Chapter 3
LET'S GET PHYSICAL...

The idea of being healthy and fit as it relates to Leadership is not a new idea or concept. In fact, leaders who are physically active and viewed as "fit" are viewed as more effective in their leadership capacities (Kearney, Campbell, & McDowell-Larsen, 2002), and while I agree that being healthy and fit can help leaders, I believe it's less about improving and rather about helping to eliminate decline.

Let me explain. Let's say I rate myself a solid 8 on a scale of 1-10 as a leader, employee, contributor, husband, dad, etc. Not bad, right? I would take an 8, awesome. (Not sure if I am an 8 but just go with it). This 8 is comprised of my results at work, how my children value our time together, how may honey dos I have knocked out on the list, and so on. Eight is our baseline. Now let's say our baseline includes morning walks, being active, eating healthy, and a generally active and healthy lifestyle. Then it changes. Instead of bringing lunch to work you eat at the local fast food restaurant. You go to bed later, wake up later, and miss your morning walks. (plus, it's hot out so who needs that)? Now you put on a few pounds but no biggie you can buy some new clothes. Your energy level decreases, therefore there is no time for those honey dos (you will get to them later). Even your sleep does not seem as restful because your energy is lower than before. You start to lose confidence, which effects your performance. I could go on but I think you get the picture. A general level of fitness and health helps to set the BASELINE of how you perform in life. When you lose your focus and attention on it, it becomes a detractor to your life. Instead of looking at your physical health as an enhancer to your life, (which it certainly can be) its absence can be a significant detractor from your basic baseline.

I have found that those who take fitness to the next level possess the types of traits that can excel in business. I believe this is derived from a handful of factors. The first is the presence of discipline. Have you met those super fit people I am speaking of? I recently had a boss who was an ultra-competitive cyclist and completed multiple cycling events per year. This was beyond the normal "regular exercise and diet;" this guy was an exceptional athlete. This was a component of who he was and it worked for him. I believe it worked for him because he tapped into something he needed. He loved the competitive nature of cycling and it was an outlet for him to compete as well as maintain and improve his health. Plus, it was difficult, as it required the discipline to make long rides, to train, and to eat a certain diet. This discipline and commitment can help propel a different version of discipline and commitment in the workplace. An added benefit is that his training and excellence inspired others, which is highly beneficial to a leader's organization. This dedication to some type of physical pursuit is not for everyone and it requires time and effort but I would be remiss if I did not at least reflect on the ultra-fit, so if you are a cross fitter keep hitting the tire with sledge hammers. No matter the intensity of your exercise program a little bit of fitness can go a long way.

Get your rest

The idea of sleep has been studied extensively (Rosekind, et al., 2010). Sleep could be referenced in a couple areas of this book but I left it within the physical space as it has been discussed as the requirement for both physical and mental excellence. Basically, sleep is far more important than society views it. We live in a world where we are often going at hundreds of miles an hour and proper sleep can take a back seat. This was especially true for me when I was younger. Staying out late, waking up too early, exposing yourself to too much screen time prior to bedtime can all negatively impact your sleep patterns (Brain Basics: Understanding Sleep, 2017).

In my experience, the best sleep is the result of consistency. I have found that when I go to bed within the same hour or so each night and wake up within the same hour (even on weekends) I feel rested and ready to take on the day.

I realize that with travel and special occasions this could make it difficult. If a consistent bedtime is difficult try to at least meet the minimum requirement of hours you need. For me my minimum amount of sleep to be effective is five and a half hours. This is not my ideal but any less and I am far less effective. Seven hours per night appears to be my optimal sleeping amount, which I attempt to meet each day. I found what seems to be optimal on my own but some people work with professionals to help determine the most effective time. Here is the deal for this section. We all have busy lives and often we are unable to get the type of sleep we want. Control what you can control. Turn off the TV, the video game, Facebook app, whatever. If you are sabotaging your own sleep with distractions you are *sabotaging your success* and making it difficult to rebound when you do have unavoidable situations that make sleep difficult.

Rest continued
but really more about productivity

Believe it or not I have a bit more about rest and sleep… more specifically take care of what you can before you go to bed. Try to put out your clothes, make your lunch, your kids' lunch. The more you can offload your mind before hitting the sack the easier it will be to fall asleep (Walton, 2018). You may have the type of mind that constantly wanders and worries, and having multiple things to take care of in the morning does not make sleep any easier. Also, you will make better food choices (instead of grabbing a hamburger from a fast food restaurant), and your clothes are more likely to match when you are not scrambling to get the kids dressed and fed while picking out socks or a tie. I think this is it on this sleep subject, now go to bed.

What about starting the day?

How you wake up matters. For most of my life I have awoken to an alarm. You all know the type the very loud BEEP!!BEEP!!!BEEP!!! It startles you as you struggle to find the snooze or off button, often stumbling around as if your bedroom has somehow been replaced by a maze of shoes and clothing on the floor, as well as the occasional "hot wheel." Waking up should not feel like someone has broken into your home and you are scrambling to take on the intruder. If you are still using a Klaxon-like device replace it with something gentler. I use a free app on my smart phones that is not so shocking but still does the trick. It allows me to get up much more naturally and ready to begin my day.

A bit about mornings or whenever you wake up

Mornings can be incredibly powerful. I once read that the vast majority of successful CEOs wake up before 6 a.m. So, I have now set my alarm for 5:59 a.m. for several years. Hey, one minute is one minute. The idea of waking up early (I realize early is different depending on when you start your work day) is meant to help improve your consistency in spending a certain amount of time each day alone. Spending committed time alone can have tremendously beneficial effects. Most leaders I know are surrounded by people the majority of the day. When they are at work it is often a day full of conference calls, meetings, requests, and so on. Quiet moments at the beginning of the day to get your thoughts together and help you prepare can be extremely helpful. It helps you take on the more intense part of your day with a greater focus and the ability to be engaged.

A tip on being present

It is extremely important to be fully engaged and present during the day. One of the areas of the day I would most often lose a bit of my engagement is during larger meetings and/or conference calls. Whether it was zoning out or checking my phone I often viewed the meetings as a waste of time. And, I must admit, I need to read my own book here, as I still sometimes find my mind wandering... however, I am improving. I improved by beginning to change the perspective I had on meetings and reviewing my *presence perspective*. I began to attend the meetings with the idea that no matter what meeting it was, it was my meeting. It was my meeting in the context that I was attending the meeting in order to receive information that would help me and my business. I would go in order to seek information, ask questions, and garner from the group potential assets and information that would make my team and I more successful. I also encouraged my teams and peers, and whomever would listen, that they should attend meetings with the same approach. How can they gain from the meeting as opposed to simply listening and delivering information? When one attends with the idea of asking questions and seeking information it will require dialogue and information sharing that is useful and needed. This simple mindset shift has helped tremendously in not only my attention span but the success of my teams as well.

Back to the physical activity stuff

I tend to spend about 30 to 45 minutes most mornings doing some type of exercise. This usually is a combination of weight training and cardiovascular activity. Again, as I previously mentioned, I am far from extremely fit, however, I am generally healthy and active. If you want an idea to creating a habit with a level of actual interest, this is one that I recently started using. Recently, I downloaded a Podcast that keeps my mind engaged. I am only able to listen to it during the workout. It gives me something to look forward to and it not only helps me make sure I find the time to do the exercise, it also makes the time go by much quicker. My current fiction podcast is called "We're Alive" and it is about zombies and the end of civilization. Think "Walking Dead" but done on the radio in a very theatrical method similar to radio programs of the 40s and 50s. If you are not into zombies check out the list provided by the website podcasthost.com (McLean, 2017) for other ideas on engaging Pods. With any exercise program or anything you want to do regularly and get better at, it is about creating ways to make it occur more often and with less resistance. Find your exercise sweet spot, find your story, and find it regularly.

Time to read

I try to spend 10 to 15 minutes a day reading the bible. I use the Bible App developed by my friends at Life church to find a good reading plan and I either read directly from the app or use it in conjunction with my Study Bible. I often find the combination of both paper and electronic helps balance my journey, keep me on track, and allows for greater note-taking and learning. If you have not read the Bible in its entirety, you are far from alone. I have had difficulty in the past maintaining the continuity of the stories. I recommend the reading plan titled EPIC. It has several parts and helps to put context behind each of the chapters, plus it keeps you on a logical path of reading where stories of the Bible flow. This particular plan has been one of the best ones I have ever used to help the bible make sense even through some of the more complex chapters.

If the Bible is not your thing, no problem, find something else that stimulates your mind and soul. Biographies, self-help books, leadership themed (re-read this book many times), how to play the harmonica, really it is more about quiet thoughtful reading. Take notes, reflect, and try to apply whatever the lessons are in order to make them more meaningful and real.

Quiet moments

I usually spend a bit of time in private prayer. Just me and the Lord. I think of Him as someone I can tell everything to, I celebrate Him, I ask for guidance, whatever is on my heart. On occasion I may also replace praying with a meditation, however I have found that meditation later in the day is more helpful in managing stress. It really is about where you apply your focus. Socrates once said, "The secret of change is to focus all your energy, not on fighting the old but on building the new." What I love about Socrates's quote and the quiet of my mediation\prayer practice is where we place the focus. Often, we focus our efforts on trying to change a poor behavior or eliminate something negative from our life. While there is nothing wrong with attempting to resolve issues, the best energy is spent on the creation of something more positive.

While these are *my* alone moment activities they are only examples. Each of us is different and should approach this recommendation as such. I have heard examples of people practicing an instrument, doing tai chi, watering plants, working on a story. The goal is to focus on something important to you that is not directly tied to your work day or even family. This is personal time that should be set aside for you.

Just because you are out of town

Currently, as I write this book, I am sitting in an airport returning home after a multi-day business trip. I suspect that many of you are reading this book potentially on an airplane or in an airport. I would also guess that you or someone you know has uttered the phrase, "It's hard to keep up with exercise, eating right, or my regular regimen while I travel." Yep, I agree. Different time zones, different expectations, later nights, limited access to gyms and healthy food. My recommendation is, do not completely give in to the idea of picking it up when you return. Find a new way that may be unique or creative to help keep up with what you do. Continue to choose healthy options if possible, do your best to hit the hotel gym, pool, or potentially go for a walk. I realize this is easier said than done but travel should not be an excuse. I have found in my own experience and in speaking with others, often the biggest culprit in a business travel to hijacking routine is the overindulgence of alcohol and poor eating. Studies show those who travel often report poor self-rated health, increased smoking, trouble sleeping, greater dependence on alcohol, higher body mass indexes (BMI), and greater risk of cardiovascular disease (Rundle, 2018). We have to work to be responsible when traveling and the more we can be cognizant of the potential challenges the greater the opportunity to sustain a healthy lifestyle. Remember, you are not on vacation. Work trips should remain as work trips.

Using work travel effectively

The majority of work trips are designed to either come together to collaborate and build relationships, or potentially learn develop and grow. They are not designed to have individuals completely cut loose and lose focus on the successful tactics that they employ at home as it relates to physical health. You can still enjoy yourself and not come off as the stuffy weirdo who is no fun, just limit it. Be an example, conduct yourself professionally, and it will be received well. While staying up late and being part of the crew closing down the lobby bar may seem to be fun, and heck "Bob from Accounting" is on his fifth Dewar's, it is not a good idea. You are reading this book to become more successful and a more effective leader, correct? Well, being an example to others, even if you think no one is paying attention, is part of that equation. Plus, if you get back to the room at a decent hour you are much more likely to wake up to complete the travel version of your routine.

Additionally, I have found, for me personally, it is important to try to catch my son before he goes to sleep so I can tell him goodnight. Depending on whether you have children or not do not forget that as a parent you are still a family leader when away. That leadership often requires taking the time when traveling to make your children feel important and cared for. I will end this particular section with a last thought. When you travel and you watch people, especially leaders, are you more impressed with Sara from marketing who is up early doing her morning jog prior to the meeting or Bob from accounting who was up late cracking wise at the bar? We have all seen our own Saras and Bobs... which one will you be?

Chapter 4
IT'S MENTAL UP IN HERE

The next area of importance is mental strength and development. Often, as leaders, we get to a place in our lives where we become somewhat stagnant in our own development and mental stimulation. Engaging your mind has tremendous benefits; in fact, mental stimulation has been shown to be an essential pillar to reducing your risk of developing Alzheimer's (Smith, Melinda, Robinson, & Segal, 2018) The greatest leaders I have met are those who continue their personal mental development and learning. This learning has been a long one for me, and since this is my book I will share a bit of my educational experience.

Education, whether truly academic or not, is vital. As a child, higher education was something I was not sure I would need and I thought I would not have the capacity to succeed in a University environment. I recall being a relatively poor student who struggled mightily in elementary school through high school graduation. This was especially true in mathematics.

When I look back now I can see breakdowns on why I did not excel early on. The biggest was poor habits. I was a constant procrastinator and often found myself doing homework on the way to school as opposed to well before deadlines. I was often bored in classes and would find my mind wandering as opposed to focusing on the teacher or the lesson. How much of my poor habits were influenced by troubles at home I cannot say, but what I can say, the items that I could control, getting enough sleep, (this guy and this sleep thing again), studying during times I had open, and seeking help when I needed it, I did not do often enough.

While my grades were nothing to be too impressed by I did tend to apply real effort to areas I was interested in. Clubs and athletics are where I spent much of my time at school and because of my extracurricular activity I was able to survive high school and ultimately completed high school which was a long-awaited accomplishment.

Upon completion of high school, I attended a local community college, but once again lost the focus and interest in my studies. I am not sure I had healed from the passing of my father when I was sixteen in order to give college the type of commitment and attention it required. Another route had been on my mind for a few years and once it was clear college was not for me I joined the military. Specifically, the United States Air Force.

The Air Force was an essential and challenging portion of my life and a period of time in which I learned many aspects of life far beyond what I may have learned if I immediately went to college. Areas such as discipline, self-control, serving others, honor, and respect. These were all aspects of my life that were enhanced and hardened. The Air Force also does place a high level of emphasis on education, and it had partnerships, through the community college of the Air Force, with dozens of Universities across the country. These partnerships allowed me to take one of my first college classes in a tent with 15 or so other airmen in Saudi Arabia while I was deployed there supporting operations associated with Operation Desert Storm.

These classes in the middle of the desert in a tent with a bunch of smelly, tired airman was the catalyst I needed to start an educational experience that would continue for decades. If you can learn about Humanities in 120-degree heat in the middle of nowhere after working straight for three days, you can take a class anywhere. Fast forward 25 years and thousands of hours' worth of formal and informal education and I sit here now with four college degrees one of which represents a PhD with honors. With all of that said, here is the main point of this section. Always be learning!

I am goal-oriented and I figured the education and degrees would help with my career and my ability to teach others, and it has done that. However, more importantly, it required me to engage my mind and to continuously learn about things that I was either not familiar with or areas I needed to continue to expand. That is what I am trying to express here. It is great to get a formal education and if that is an option you should certainly do that. However, what is really important is to continue to learn and educate yourself. *If you are not learning you are losing.* These learning pursuits can be formal through a university or self-driven through books, webcasts, podcasts, music lessons, martial arts, whatever. It does not matter, just challenge your mind and learn something.

A mindful life

During my doctorial journey I searched for many topics to study. I was all over the place. I went from wanting to study the influence of music on church growth to stress management and how companies are dealing with employee burn out, to the potential study of one leader I found to be uniquely successful. Through all of the research, I could never quite land on something so I thought I would do two things. Be a significant contribution to the academic community while teaching me something I could apply to my own leadership life. What I found was an interesting phenomenon... the idea of mindfulness was beginning to pop up all over corporate America. In fact, many of my own offices were beginning to create "quiet rooms" that allowed for meditation. As I unpacked this I became interested in meditation myself beyond the dissertation.

Studies have shown that mindfulness helps to decrease negative stress, heighten focus, improve memory, and the list went on. In the research I also found that many business leaders who faced anxiety and depression related issues were alleviated by mindful practice (Davis & Hayes, 2011). I was one of those leaders and have dealt with depression and anxiety much of my life.

With all of that in mind I searched for my first book related to mindfulness and found *The Power of Now* by Eckhart Tolle. This powerful book helped to highlight that within our lives we can truly only focus on now. We cannot change the past or control the future, therefore *the now is what we need to work on*. This is not to say we are not to prepare for the future or learn from mistakes but rather make today matter. Put each moment into focus and apply your best effort to what you are currently engaged in.

This simple idea helped to open me up to a whole new world related to being more mindful and how to apply meditation to my life. I also found that many successful people I worked with and admired built meditation into their lives. Meditation has been shown to increase brain function and the ability for neurons to transmit more effectively (Jang, Jung, Byun, & Kang, 2010). Meditation is simple to do and the time can be limited to nearly as short as you like.

I try to do 10 to 15 minutes a day. I utilize an app called CALM, which is a guided meditation. In my experience, a midday meditation is helpful in resetting me, especially if a day has been hectic or stressful. I often recall a quote about stillness and the power it can generate. *Lao Tzu says, "be still like a mountain and flow like a great river."* Powerful and so true. I am much more productive once I settle my mind and dial in my focus. You might have attempted to work meditation into your day but find it difficult to keep it consistent. It is worth the effort but meditation does take time to pay off; it is not measurable immediately. However, imagine if I were to tell you that for only 10 minutes a day you could increase your memory, improve your ability to perform, increase happiness, and the list goes on... would you agree to it? Very few things are able to provide so many benefits in so little time.

On occasion, I still have to psyche myself up to fit in the time to meditate. I become a more effective thinker when I regularly complete mindfulness exercises. Therefore, taking the time to meditate for 10 minutes pays off in dividends.

One easy illustration of the power of meditation is in the increase of short-term memory capacity. A quick little experiment you can do is to take some index cards and write down a series of single and double-digit numbers. Start with a stack of 15 or so. Then flip through the cards looking at each for no longer than one second. Once you are done jot down the numbers you recall in order. The average person recalls five to nine numbers in order (McLeod, 2009).

This is a rough estimation of your current short-term memory capacity. Record that number, then commit to a solid four weeks of regular mediation and then complete the index card flash card test again.

While I cannot guarantee that it will show an increase I suspect it will based on my own experience and improvements made by those I have shared this with previously. Increased short-term memory allows you to recall information faster, process information faster, retain more information, and the ability to work on multiple tasks and or projects. In a nutshell, short-term memory is awesome! *Short*-term memory can go a *long* way.

Culture of your life

Often, we consider culture as either a part of the broader society in which we live and/or the environment we are managing within our organizations. We may have read books about culture and how to continue to improve or maintain. For the purpose of this book and how culture plays a role in personal leadership and development I encourage the reader to look at culture locally within your own world. What type of culture do you have at home, how do you interact with your family, friends, co-workers, neighbors?

We influence our own culture wherever we are.

The culture that you contribute to and shape are the baselines for how you will interact in your world. Like it or not, you are and will be heavily influenced by the culture you surround yourself in. If the culture is weak or negative those two items will seep into your professional life. Conversely, by attempting to surround yourself in a culture of positivity and strength you will also be influenced. Either way, a culture will exist, you have a choice to influence it so do so. No one gets to be a non-participant in culture, *culture is contagious and contingent.* It will spread no matter what and its direction is contingent on the behaviors and focus of leaders within that culture. All leaders need to be cognizant on their tremendous influence on culture, stay aware, and engaged.

Chapter 5
DRIVING RESULTS

This book is designed to both provide guidance on general productivity and success of individual leaders, however I would like to also spend some time on a leader's role in driving results. Much of what I have discussed has been focused inward. This is the most important step of any endeavor. How can we improve, train, focus or enhance our own perspective or ability in order to create a better world, workplace, home? Now I would like to discuss a very tactical approach to driving results that are meaningful and sustainable.

Understand where you want to be

Far too often, we push for more results with the goal to simply achieve "more" or move "faster;" really the vague descriptor does not matter. "Just keep doing what you're doing but do it better." We may not say it that bluntly but when goals and targets are vague that is basically what winds up happening. To simply say that we want to "improve" or "get better," while conceptually true, are not specific enough.

There must be a north star of sorts. If it is difficult to understand the potential end result you can use short-term targets as a measurement to go towards.

I look at achieving results in a very linear fashion. This linear method looks at a result, metric, goal, or project in a similar manner to how one would solve an algebraic equation. These are known variables and unknown variables. To begin you must decide what those variables represent. Typically, these variables revolve around resources and outcomes. Resources could be financial, personnel, time, and so on. The outcomes consist of goals that are measurable and represent the efforts of the work. Everything involved in creating your equation to success is either an input or an output. Once you understand the potential components, you can then begin to build your equation.

Begin by clearly identifying the resources. Examples include personnel involved, financial resources, systems or processes. Then try to identify what else could be needed and plug those variables in. Lastly, list out the intended goals or potential goals. Let's say you want to increase the retention of employees. First, you can identify the goal by understanding the current state. For the purpose of this example let's state that the current attrition number each month is the loss of five employees. You have a workforce that is 100 people. That represents a 5% monthly attrition rate or potentially 60% (5 times 12 months) turnover each year. Now let's identify an achievable improvement of reducing from an average of five employees each month down to four employees a month. This would represent now 4% per month and an annualized attrition of 48%. Now we have an end result that we can build an equation toward.

We should look now at what are the contributing factors of attrition. Items such as compensation, hours, culture, and leadership. We can define each of these and analyze. Compensation equates to X, the hours of employees equates to Y, leadership equals L, and recognition equates to M. The equation would look something like:

Appropriate compensation + shift and hours + culture of the work place + leadership effectiveness = improved attrition.

With this equation we can now begin to solve the equation by identifying the lowest common denominators that have positive influence to the most factors.

A potential common denominator for this example might be leadership training on how to effectively use performance spiffs or reward and recognition. In this training you could address leadership effectiveness, the value of some type of spiff program, and how it can be leveraged a bit more aggressively during shifts that are less than favorable. This training and then the implementation of the rewards program addresses each of the areas we determined to be impacting attrition. Spiffs and rewards can be viewed as an element of compensation and using these rewards more effectively may improve the perception of compensation.

By utilizing them a bit more aggressively during shifts that are viewed as less favorable or having higher turnover you are able to address potential negative viewpoints on certain shifts. Culture can be enhanced when employees are effectively rewarded and leadership effectiveness can certainly be improved and bolstered during the training itself.

This activity that views a problem or goal through the lens of an algebraic equation provides a solid, concrete task that can be worked on that has the potential to improve multiple areas of the equation. This "lowest common denominator" work should continue until results are achieved and the equation is clear and captured. We ensure that we not only do the work but we also capture the equation so we know how to implement if similar future challenges or goals are determined. This allows for greater speed to a solution and it provides the blueprint for other leaders to utilize, and in many cases improve upon during future endeavors.

A different approach to the lowest common denominator

If you allow me to go back to personnel development again this method of lowest common denominator can also be applied to personal goals and direction. This method allows us to compartmentalize areas to focus on. If you are reading this you are likely looking to improve in some way. This improvement can be far beyond simple leadership. The *Lowest Common Denominator* approach can be used for nearly everything.

For example, say you are having trouble with your weight. This seems to be a common area many people are focusing on. I am writing about this during the month of January and I have seen more people at my gym than I have ever seen and I have heard at least twelve conversations relating to diet, particularly "fasting." Let's take that one as our example and apply our lowest common denominator theory. First, we define the goal or what we want our equation to solve. In this case we can state "the loss of 10 lbs and reducing body fat by 5%." With this in mind we can then begin to reverse engineer the solution.

Obviously, two major components are diet and exercise... yes, I know you know that but let's dig deeper. If we begin to solve them both we find that we need to find the time to exercise and we need to reduce our reliance on fast food or eating out in general. We are now closer to the lowest common denominator, which is something to do with "time." We peel that down even further and find that we have no time because we are always running out of the house and it is difficult to make it to work on time due to rush hour. Hence, we have trouble not stopping for food on the way in, and then by the time we get to work we are a bit stressed and start our day off on the wrong foot, so what does it really matter that my day is already shot because I ate poorly on the way in, I had no time in the morning to work out and then the spiral continues.

The lowest common denominator in this case could be preparation in the morning. Solve that and you create time, which allows for the ability to eat better in the morning, potentially find an alternative route to work, potentially change your hours at work a couple of minutes. This is only a figurative example but I think you get the picture... we often focus on the macro but miss the micro of the equation. In this case, if we created 20 minutes in the morning we might be able to prepare a healthier option for breakfast and maybe take a walk. This portion of the equation, time, specifically time in the morning, has a positive influence on both diet and exercise and gets us one step closer to the ultimate goal, which we stated above.

Chapter 6
INFLUENCE OF MOOD

The moods of coworkers have tremendous influence on the effectiveness of our teams and can be influenced by many different contributors (Barsade & Gibson, 2007). Sleep (there it is again), food or lack thereof (hunger), personal relationships, and the list goes on.

We already discussed the idea of emotional intelligence (EI) and understanding the element of mood on behavior and interactions. This EI should certainly be considered, especially when making decisions or having impactful conversations.

A couple of tips that we should know. Mood is often improved when someone comes off vacation, (yeah, no kidding), however by simply thinking about timing you are often in a better position to get an answer you may prefer. So, consider that when you are thinking about asking your boss about the next promotion, raise, budget increase for a project. Boss never goes on vacation? How about after their team wins a big game, something great happens in the business, their child gets accepted to college. The idea is not to manipulate or try to "trick" someone into doing something they do not want to do but rather trying to improve the odds.

This can be also understood at home. I fully appreciate the influence of moods in my family, including my own. Often families have to discuss important and sometimes difficult conversations. Timing is important if you want to have conversations that limit the amount of emotional influence. Leaders should use this knowledge when engaging others.

Conversations that matter

Conversations Count. Much of what we do with communication today relies on some type of social or *minimalist interaction.* A tweet, an Instagram, a snap, a quick IM, or even email. The actual verbal communication between two people has been reduced. The ability to have a good conversation and the ability to guide a meaningful dialogue can be skillset that sets you apart.

Conversational threading is a method that can help with that. It builds on the idea of personal storytelling and connection. Conversational threading is a fairly new concept for me but one that has begun to help me have more meaningful conversations. It helps break down barriers and improves connectivity (not the 4G kind) during interactions.

It works like this. In the beginning of virtually any conversation try to pick up one or two themes that you can expand on. For example, you might ask an open-ended question such as, "Wow, on the way into work today it was stop and go and my navigation took me a completely different route. What was your commute like?" Now this can be a closed response but likely it allows the type of open dialogue about a subject both parties had to deal with. The other individual is at work, therefore they needed to get here, and therefore they had some sort of commute. Now let's say your coworker responds, "It wasn't too bad. Today, I had to drop my son off at school because my wife is traveling so I left a little earlier than normal, which helped me beat some of the rush." This is where the threading comes into play... are you ready?

"It was not too bad. Today, I had to drop my son off at school because my wife is traveling so I left a little earlier than normal, which helped me beat some of the rush."

There are a few different "threads" to pull upon. 1. Dropping son off at school, 2. Wife is traveling, 3. Beating the rush hour. From there you can begin a more in-depth conversation with a threaded reply. "I love beating rush hour, it makes the travel so much smoother. When I lived in Chicago it was even worse, as I would have to leave at like 4 a.m. to beat it. What is the worst and best city you have ever driven in as far as traffic?" Now we have the beginning of a conversation that can go back and forth and build upon each other in order to create a better connection and enhance rapport.

You can use this in nearly all situations and it can be extremely helpful when the intent of the conversation is ultimately a difficult subject. Start a *conversation with connectivity* it helps to ensure the message gets across.

Sustaining results

How about we discuss developing structure that allows for sustained performance? Each individual you have the opportunity to lead is very unique and has skills, talents, and experience that has helped to define them. Because each is unique it is important to understand both strengths and weaknesses so you are better able to define parameters for how to conduct business.

Many employees need very little oversight and

can operate with a substantial amount of flexibility and self-guidance. However, many individuals need greater structure and this difference can be illustrated by what I call the Sphere of Excellence. While I sometimes struggle with creating visuals, allow me to illustrate.

If you can imagine the sun as the center of the universe. This sun represents the process and procedures either identified by the organization or as defined by the appropriate leadership personnel. This could be steps on a checklist, guidelines on how to complete projects, scripting, basically anything that can be referenced for step-by-step expectations of what an employee should do. Very clear, very little room for misinterpretation and/or personal adaptation or nuance. Those needing the most direction and instruction can be viewed as the closest planets, as they need to stay close in order to not lose their orbit around the sun and leave their correct place within the solar system. As you work your way away from the sun other planets can be found that have different gravitational needs.

These differences dictate how well a planet is able to rotate around the sun. If we expand to the galaxy aspect of the analogy we then can see the larger picture with each planet circling the sun at its own speed and orbit. This solar system can be described as the acceptable level of performance or even better said not only acceptable but a term we could call the *spheres of excellence.*

The key idea here being that each planet or (person) requires the right amount of centrifugal force and gravity. If there is not enough centrifugal force (support and motivation) and gravity (development and tools) the employee or planet can jettison out into space losing the ability to return and also negatively impacting the rest of the solar system. With all of this said sometimes it is just easier to see it:

Spheres of Excellence

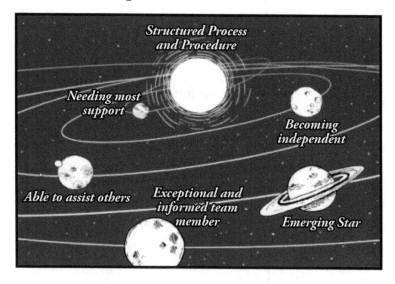

Chapter 7
SUSTAIN YOUR DIRECTION

Sooner or later everyone faces a rut. It happens in nearly everything, from professional sports to the executive office. Ruts are a fact, however, a rut as defined is:

- A long deep track made by the repeated passage of the wheels of vehicles.
  synonyms: furrow, groove, trough, ditch, hollow, pothole, crater
  "the car bumped across the ruts."

- a habit or pattern of behavior that has become dull and unproductive but is hard to change.

  "the administration was stuck in a rut and was losing its direction."
  synonyms: boring routine, humdrum existence, habit, dead end
  "he was stuck in a rut."

Wow, ruts are exactly what they sound like! The first definition a long deep track made by the repeated passage of the wheels of a vehicle. Hmm… when I consider this one I am drawn by the word "repeated." As I reflect, I think whether or not ruts are deeper and harder to get out of the more we repeat them. The second definition *"stuck in the rut"* and commentary around losing direction "dead end" "boring routine" speak to the feelings you feel while stuck in one. So, what to do?

First, let's digest the definition. Ruts occur when repeated activities (like tires) drive on the same path thereby creating the rut. So, on the emotional and metaphysical level ruts would also seem to be created in the same manner. As we do the same things, day in and day out, we may become bored. Think about this for a moment… even in this book I speak about the importance of discipline and routine. Prepare your food and clothing, wake up around the same time each day, exercise, eat healthy, go to work, drive results, engage with employees, etc, etc.

I and many others speak about the power of repetition and how that repetition can increase effectiveness and skill. I still believe that repetition and structure to your day and week are important but I do also want to consider the potential impact of creating ruts.

Repeated activity, day in and day out can potentially influence the likelihood of boredom. I have run into this many times; in fact, as I write this I might be in a bit of one. I have found that I fall victim of the *"rut rundown"* when I am not challenging myself. Doing the same thing every day in and out, that's the obvious one.

The other area that may cause a rut quickly is avoiding things that scare you. Something that is outside of your comfort zone. This means to do something that often you are not very good at or have never accomplished before. I don't necessarily mean doing skydiving (although that would fit the bill) but potentially something new or interesting that you can build into your current days and processes.

For example, maybe you would like to improve team communication, so why not add a new method of delivery for communications to your next team meeting, by learning about a new web-based video share software? I know that may sound lame but when you learn something new, that can help your team, it really does make a difference to reduce the potential *"rut strut."* You know the "rut strut" going through the motions but not being as engaged as you would like. You wake up knowing what you are supposed to do and then do a version of that, but it is only a facsimile of what you know it could be. It is not until you find the passion or inspiration that you rebound from the "rut strut" and begin pouring into your work again.

Now, of course, each of us is different and the regularity of the rut strut is unique to each of us but rest assured that when you are in the "*rut strut*" you can still get out. Again, there are tricks to jumping out, the aforementioned challenge or something you fear, as well as finding a new potential love or passion.

If you are anything like me it can be easier to find that area of life that you fear or view as a challenge than to find the next love or passion. If this is the case for you as well, here is an idea of sorts to help pick up a new passion.

This one takes some peace and quiet so find a place you can sit by yourself, with a pen and paper. Now think to yourself. You have just won the lottery, making work a non-necessity for yourself and your children (of course, many of us would still work, but play along with me). Now you have all the money you need in the world. Your time is also almost unlimited meaning your commitments, restraints, time consuming tasks no longer exist. So you have unlimited, time, money, resources, and support.

Take a minute and really let that sink in... your life is void of any essential need or time constraint. With that in mind, what would you do, what would you like to be involved in?

As the ideas pop into your head write them down. Even if they don't seem to make sense, write them down. After some time and you feel like everything that could have come out of your quiet consideration has come out, take a break.

Come back to the list a couple days later and then begin to determine how you can introduce elements of the list into your current world. If its charity, organize a food drive at work and then drop it off on a Saturday with family. If its teaching, change the way you conduct your one-on-ones and focus more on development and training as opposed to performance review. The list goes on but find a way to bring a new interest into your current role and life, as this helps to *repair the rut!*

The life event

I have not worked out in three weeks. I have not gotten a good night's rest in over a month. My wife and I barely have time to even give the fleeting glance of romance. I have missed church more than I have gone. My 3-year-old has watched more TV in the last month than he has most of his life. I have missed a lot of work. My work colleagues are picking up a lot of the slack concerning work I am not doing. Writing this book has not been a priority; in fact, this is the first time I have written anything in over two weeks. I had to file an extension on my taxes. My showering habits remind me of my adolescence in that I often forget to even take one. I am a complete mess... BUT, I am also incredibly happy and blessed.

My wife just had a baby.... I say my wife not only because it is indeed a fact, I was only a witness not the bearer of the baby, but also because it is indeed an act to be recognized. Having a baby is the culmination of about ten months of work followed by a varied level of effort, pain, struggle, and purpose. Each birth obviously is unique to the woman, however from my vantage point, my wife should have some kind of bracelet or t-shirt signifying the accomplishment. You know the ones I am talking about. Like the Spartan headband and t-shirt, Tough Mudders, some random cross-fit endurance pain fest. Or at least a bumper sticker similar to those marathon runners or half marathon 13.1 stickers. I can only provide my perspective as I have definitely have not been pregnant or had a baby, but damn girl, you go.

Back to me not doing anything that I normally do, because obviously my family has had a wonderful HUGE change. I am still in the midst of it but thought it was appropriate to add this to the book as everyone has some type of huge change that can require the flexibility to adapt in order to maintain momentum and direction.

Having the ability to be flexible in the way you manage your life during this time is important. During the first few months after your baby arrives stress is at elevated levels (Seah & Morawska, 2016). You can easily allow the stress to overwrite the joy if you are not careful.

I also know that much of my book is spent specifically focusing on "you" the individual. That is the purpose and yes that is where a lot of focus should be. How can I become a better leader, person, family member, and the list goes on? However, I also know that as dynamics at home change, responsibilities increase, and your focus begins to ebb and flow between your own personal development and the development of say… your children, you likely have less time, resources, and capacity.

With all of this change I was going to say you must simply approach it as a "season of life."

Literally, that was going to be my message here. I would go into the temporary adjustment period and that in due time you would return to a period of "normalcy." This idea of "seasons" has been a concept I have heard many times and one that I could speak to. Then boom...! This week I saw a post from my friend Bobby Gruenwald who is one of the lead pastors for LIFE church and also a co-creator of the Bible app.

I saw that he posted in his LinkedIn feed a brief idea that he was eliminating the phrase "this is just a season." In his statement he discussed that by claiming "it is only a season" it sets the idea that whatever it is will at some point end, which may or may not occur and also can set an incorrect expectation. It also likely causes you to delay or hold off on things you might normally work toward due to the fact that you believe the situation might significantly change.

This one incredibly insightful statement changed my approach to this idea of "seasons." In the particular situation I am currently in, it is less of a situation and more a fantastic life event; having another child. I have changed my mindset from one that focuses less on the change of situation but rather the adaptation I must make in order to be more effective during the situation. I have deemed this idea as implementing "*temporary tactics.*"

This idea of temporary tactics has a similar idea of how a leader would adjust to the situation, i.e., in Situational Leadership theory. The leader must adjust his style, approach, and methods in order to better match the situation that he or she faces (Hersey & Blanchard, 1977). One of the most common major changes to a situation are when significant life events occur and your time becomes even more limited or you have to adjust a schedule significantly enough that your typical routine gets turned upside down. The recommendation, and I am still working through it myself, is to implement the "temporary tactic."

Let's say, for example, that you used to wake up early several days a week in order to train, go to the gym, what have you. Now you are up several times in the evening with a baby waking up early it is not logical as you need to cram in every second of sleep in you can. The temporary tactic play is to start with the goal of the activity you are missing and then work your way backwards to a new tactic to help achieve that goal. In this particular situation the idea is personal fitness. Therefore, I must find alternatives or "temporary tactics" to reach the goal.

When developing a tactic, you must first understand the full change of situation. My main change is a reduction of sleep and an increase in walking around with a ten-pound baby weight. So, the temporary tactic is, whenever I walk around with the baby I do so with a dual purpose. Soothing the baby is number one, but also trying to make up some type of physical activity to offset the lack of gym time. We walk around laterally, fast then slow, we do squats, and lunges. Walking with the baby can look ridiculous but the honest truth is, so far it isn't a bad alternative for a mix of cardio and a lower body workout.

My older son, who is three, is accustomed to me coming home from work and often doing something more sedentary, such as reading books, coloring, playing on the floor with his superheroes (on a side note, how did superheroes take over, like everything)? Now when I get home our activities are much more physical: swimming in the pool, playing tag, or going to the park where we take turns on the monkey bars. I realize this is not some major epiphany for many of you, however I include it here to take a moment to recognize the conscious decision to introduce a *temporary tactic* as opposed to complete elimination of an element associated with the Physical, Mental or Spiritual aspect of your life.

Wrapping it all up

When I began writing this book, I set out to provide some insight and detail around helping you to become a better leader. I felt that it was important to give structure and concepts that would not only make sense but allow for some real world practicality that you can introduce into your own life. The ideas and processes in this book related to the balance of Physical, Mental and Spiritual life are meant to help move the needle a little bit at a time.

Life can be difficult, wonderful, challenging, interesting, painful, inspiring, and so on. There are no simple answers to becoming our best self. We may never actually get there; I, like you, am still on this journey. I do believe though that the journey is one that is completed using small steps. Take these small steps each day to build a beautiful path of small improvements and efforts. Getting just a little better each day takes commitment and effort but everyone can do it. No matter who we are, no matter how different or alike, one thing we share is a desire to be that person who is more complete and more fulfilled. The type of person who leaves a mark on the world.

The type of person whose story will continue long after we leave this world. The type of person who is moving toward something that is amazing. What that something is may not be known but what is known is that on the way to "something" you must move… you must progress… you must put in the effort to become… JUST A LITTLE BETTER EVERYDAY.

WORKS CITED

(2015, Jan). *Nonprofit World*, p. 20.

Achor, S. (2010). *The Happiness Advantage*. Crown Publishing Group.

Angell, R., Gorton, M., Sauer, J., Bottomley, P., & White, J. (2016). Don't Distract Me When I'm Media Multitasking: Toward a Theory for Raising Advertising Recall and Recognition. *Journal of Advertising*, 198-210.

Barsade, S., & Gibson, D. (2007). Why Does Affect Matter in Oranizations? *Academy of Management Perspectives*.

Biro, M. M. (2014, February 9). *Let Love Insprire Your Leadership*. Retrieved from forbes.com: https:// www.forbes.com/sites/meghanbiro/2014/02/09/ let-love-inspire-your-leadership/#abb5436f52f9

Brain Basics: Understanding Sleep. (2017, May 22). Retrieved from National Institute of Neurological Disorders and Stroke: https://www.ninds.nih. gov/Disorders/Patient-Caregiver-Education/ Understanding-Sleep

Brewer, J. A. (2010). Mindfulness-based treatments for co-occurring depression and substance use disorders: What can we learn from the brain? *Addiction*, 1698-1706.

Brown, A., & Lahey, J. (2015). Small Victories: Creating Intrinsic Motivation in Task Completion and Debt Repayment. *Journal of Marketing Research (JMR)*, 768-783.

Cohen, M. (2016). Singularity of Thought: A Correlative Study of the Mindfulness of Senior Telecommunication Executives and Their Perceived Leadership Style.

Dasa, P., & Brendel, D. (2017, April). Does Mindfulness Training Have Business Benefits? *HR Magazine*, pp. 24-25.

Davis, D., & Hayes, J. (2011). What are the Benefits of Mindfulness? A Practice Review of Psychotherapy-Related Research. *Psychotherapy*, 198-208.

Fine, D. (2017). 4 Reasons Bosses Should Encourage Meditation. *Credit Union Management*, 8.

Fischetti, M. (2011, Nov). Computers vs. Brains. *Scientific American*, p. 104.

Ganz, S., & Hassett, K. (2008). Little League, Huge Effect. *American*, 64-67.

Goler, L., Gale, J., Harrington, B., & Grant, A. (2018, February 20). *The 3 Things Employees Really Want: Career, Community, Cause*. Retrieved from workplace by facebook: https://hbr.org/2018/02/people-want-3-things-from-work-but-most-companies-are-built-around-only-one

Hersey, P., & Blanchard, K. (1977). *Management of Organizational Behavior: Utilizing Human Resources*. New Jersey: Prentice Hall.

Jang, J. H., Jung, W. H., Byun, M. S., & Kang, D.-H. (2010). Increased default mode network connectivity associated with meditation. *Neuroscience Letters*.

Kearney, L., Campbell, D., & McDowell-Larsen, S. (2002). Fitness and leadership: is there a relationship?: Regular exercise correlates with higher leadership ratings in senior-level executives. *Journal of Managerial Psychology*, 316-324.

Kuntz, J., Malinen, S., & Naswall, K. (2017). Employee resilience: Directions for resilience development. *Consulting Psychology Journal: Practice and Research,*, 223-242.

Levitin, D. J. (2014). *The Organized Mind*. New York: Penguin Ranom House.

Maniscalco, S. (2018, March 12). Create an Authentic Word of Mouth Career. (J. Altucher, Interviewer)

Marguilies, M. (2016, June 7). Should pregnant women be induced at 39 weeks? *The Washington Post.*

McLean, M. (2017, July 1). *https://www. thepodcasthost.com/fiction-podcasts/best-audio-fiction-podcasts/.* Retrieved from The Best Fiction Podcasts: My Top 10 Audio Dramas: https://www.thepodcasthost.com/fiction-podcasts/best-audio-fiction-podcasts/

McLeod, S. (2009). *Simply Psychology.* Retrieved from Short Term Memory: https://www.simplypsychology.org/short-term-memory.html

Oakley, B. (2017). *Mindshift: Break Through Obstacles to Learning and Discover Your Hidden Potential.* New York: Penquin Random House LLC.

Rosekind, M., Gregory, K., Mallis, M., Brandt, S., Seal, B., & Lerner, D. (2010). The Cost of Poor Sleep: Workplace Productivity Loss and Associated Cost. *American College of Occupational and Environmental Medicine*, 91-98.

Rundle, A. (2018, May 31). Just How Bad is Business Travel for Your Health? Here's the Data. *Harvard Business Review.*

Seah, C. K., & Morawska, A. (2016). When Mum is Stressed, Is Dad Just as Stressed? Predictaors of Paternal Stress in the First Six Months of Having a Baby. *Infant Mental Health Journal.*

Smith, Melinda, Robinson, L., & Segal, J. (2018, March). *Preventing Alzheimer's Disease.* Retrieved from Helpguide.org: https://www.helpguide.org/articles/alzheimers-dementia-aging/preventing-alzheimers-disease.htm

Stubbs, W. (2017). Integrating For Profit and For Purpose Considerations into B Corp Business Practices. *Academy of Management Annual Meeting Proceedings.* Clayton Australia.

Turner, S. (2001). Resilience and social work practice: Three case studies. *Families in Society: The Journal of Contemporary Human Services*, 441-448.

Uwland-Sikkema, N., Visser, A., Westerhof, G., & Garssen, B. (2018). How is spirituality part of people's meaning system? *Psychology of Religion and Spirituality*, 157-165.

Walton, A. (2018, January 14). *Forbes.* Retrieved from Writing a To-Do List May Help you Fall Asleep Faster: https://www.forbes.com/sites/alicegwalton/2018/01/14/writing-before-bed-may-help-you-fall-asleep-faster/#78d4630f36f8

Warren, R. (2003). *The Purpose Driven Life.* Running Press.

White, J., Langer, E., Yariv, L., & Welch, J. (2006). Frequent Social Comparisons and Destructive Emotions. *Journal of Adult Development*, 36-43.

Wood, J. (1996). What is social comparison and how should we study it? *Personality and Social Psychology Bulletin*, 520-537.

ABOUT THE AUTHOR

Dr. Cohen has been a telecommunications executive for nearly two decades and has held senior level leadership roles for Fortune 500 companies, including Charter Communications, Comcast, United Healthcare, T-Mobile, and Dish Network. Dr. Cohen is also a Professor of Leadership and Professional Studies at Southeastern University at Celebration Church.

Beyond his business and teaching experience, Dr. Cohen has been a lifetime learner, most recently graduating from Piedmont International University with a PhD in Leadership, in 2016. In addition to his PhD, Dr. Cohen possess a Master's degree in Management, a BA in Business Communications, and an Associate's degree in Criminal Justice.

A third generation military member, Dr. Cohen is an Air Force Desert Storm era veteran. During his time in the service he supported nuclear and conventional weapon security in the US and Middle East as a member of Air Force Security Forces.

Dr. Cohen believes leadership is based on science, art, and unique God given gifts and he has studied leadership and its principles throughout his professional and academic pursuits. He has spent several years learning and applying the specialty of Leadership and recently completed a dissertation entitled "Singularity of Thought: A Correlative Study of the Mindfulness of Senior Telecommunication Executives and their Perceived Leadership Style," where he explored the influence of mindfulness on a leader's style and effectiveness.

Dr. Cohen lives in Round Rock, TX with his wife Tracy, son Noah (4 years old) and Miles (6 months old.) He also has a talented 20-year-old son Matthew who is currently continuing the service tradition as a proud member of the US Navy.